OCR HISTORY A

AS

The Unification of Italy 1815–70

Martin Collier | Series editors: Martin Collier | Rosemary Rees

£13.25

www.heinemann.co.uk

✓ Free online support
✓ Useful weblinks
✓ 24 hour online ordering

01865 888080

OCR
RECOGNISING ACHIEVEMENT

Heinemann

Official Publisher Partnership

Heinemann is an imprint of Pearson Education Limited, a company incorporated in England and Wales, having its registered office at Edinburgh Gate, Harlow, Essex, CM20 2JE. Registered company number: 872828

www.heinemann.co.uk

Heinemann is a registered trademark of Pearson Education Ltd

Text © Martin Collier 2008

12 11 10 09 08
10 9 8 7 6 5 4 3 2 1

British Library Cataloguing in Publication Data is available from the British Library on request.

ISBN 978 0 435312633

Typeset by TechType
Original illustrations © Pearson Education Limited 2008
Illustrated by TechType
Cover design by Pearson Education
Cover photo © Archivo Icongrafico, S.A./Corbis
Edited by Kirsty Taylor
Index compiled by Ian D. Crane
Printed in the UK by Henry Ling Ltd

Acknowledgements
The author and publisher would like to thank the following individuals and organisations for permission to reproduce photographs:

Museo Centrale del Risorgimento, Roma: p. 17; Bettmann/Corbis: p. 29; akg-images: p. 47; Corbis: p. 53; bpk: p. 74; Mary Evans/Mary Evans ILN Pictures; akg-images: p. 95; Museo Nazionale del Risorgimento, Turin, Italy/The Bridgeman Art Library: p. 98 (left); Hulton-Deutsch Collection/Corbis: p. 98 (right); Museo Centrale del Risorgimento, Roma: p. 106; akg-images: p. 114; Anthony P. Campanella Collection of Giuseppe Garibaldi, Thomas Cooper Library, University of South Carolina: p. 135.

Written sources
pp. 19-20 Source B: A. Saitta, Filippo Buonarroti, vol. I, Rome, 1950; p. 26 Source A: M. Clark, The Italian Risorgimento, Longman 1998; p. 59 Source E: Denis Mack Smith, The Making of Modern Italy 1798–1866, Macmillan 1968; pp. 72-73 Source A: The Survival of the Habsburg Empire by A. Sked. Reproduced by permission of Pearson Education.

Every effort has been made to contact copyright holders of material reproduced in this book. Any omissions will be rectified in subsequent printings if notice is given to the publishers.

CONTENTS

HOW TO USE THIS BOOK

The aim of this book is to give a comprehensive explanation of all the events of the *Risorgimento* and the unification of Italy. The book explains the processes by which Italy became a unified state by 1870 and the different attitudes to unification both inside and outside Italy. The emphasis of this examination unit is on historical enquiry (see also Skills). However, before students can engage in meaningful historical enquiry, they need to have a full understanding of the relevant events, issues and controversies. The book therefore follows a chronological order and outlines in detail the key issues and core content as specified by OCR.

Key Issue 1: How far did the experiences of 1815 to 1847 create support for Italian unity?

This is covered in the first three chapters of the book.

Key Issue 2: Why did the revolutions of 1848-9 in Italy fail to unite Italy?

This key issue is the focus of Chapter 4.

Key Issue 3: How important to the unification of Italy were the contributions of the Italian states (especially Piedmont and its aims) and of individuals (Cavour, Garibaldi, Mazzini and Victor Emmanuel)?

This is covered through many of the chapters, particularly Chapter 3 (Mazzini), Chapter 5 (Piedmont), Chapter 7 and 9 (Cavour) and Chapter 8 (Cavour and Garibaldi).

Key Issue 4: How important in the process of unification were foreign help and foreign circumstance?

Again, this is covered through many of the chapters but particularly in Chapters 6, 7 and 9.

Features

There are many features in the margins of the book which are directly linked to the text and will help stimulate the students' imagination and pick out key information.

Key Issues – these highlight which of the key issues of the specification is covered

Key Terms – these pick out and define key words

Key People – these give a brief biography of important people

Key Ideas – these pick out important ideas, either of the time or of historians studying this period

Key Events – these give a brief overview of important events

Key Places – these give brief explanation of why certain areas are important for this topic

Key Themes – these pick out important themes of the period

Skills

The political unification of Italy provoked considerable debate amongst contemporaries and, subsequently, amongst historians. Many of the main points of debate are explained in the book. Throughout the book students are provided with different interpretations and representations of events and issues. Students are required to demonstrate understanding through use of skills. In this book students will be:

- guided in how to evaluate critically and compare evidence,
- given an opportunity to develop in skills and knowledge, as they progress through the book, through the Enquiry style activities at the end of each chapter.

An overview of the skills required and how these can be developed from students' GCSE skills are explained in detail in the *Planning and Delivery Resource*.

Exam Café

The text in the book is supplemented by an exciting **Exam Café** feature. The Exam Café is split into three areas: Relax, Refresh, Result!

- **Relax** is a place for students to share revision tips.
- **Refresh** your memory is an area for revising content.
- **Result** provides examiner's tips and sample answers with comments.

The sample answers provided are from the questions at the end of Chapters 1 and 4.

Planning and Delivery Resource

The Unification of Italy chapter of this resource contains guidance and advice for ways to approach and teach this topic for the OCR specification. There are student worksheets which help to build up source skills for the examination requirements. This also contains lots of additional source material and an Exam Café with more tips, sample answers and detailed examiner commentary.

INTRODUCTION

Today Italy is one of the leading European states with an unrivalled richness of history and culture. But it was only as recently as 1870 that Italy was united as a nation state with Rome as its capital. However, the roots of Italian national consciousness lie before 1870 in the years of Napoleonic rule in Italy and even earlier. That stated, awareness of Italian national identity was never widespread.

The Italian peninsula in the early nineteenth century was made up of distinct political states from Lombardy, Venice and the Kingdom of Sardinia in the north, to the Kingdom of Naples in the south. It was also a patchwork of dialects and customs, ruled by Italian kings and dukes, and foreign powers. In central Italy, the Pope ruled over the Papal States.

The significance of the impact of Napoleonic rule: how French rule in Italy influenced its development for the next 60 years should not be underestimated. From 1798 until 1814, the Italian peninsula was ruled, either directly or indirectly, by Napoleon I (Napoleon Bonaparte). Although Napoleonic rule was ended by 1815 and the kings and dukes of the Italian states were restored to their thrones, French rule left its mark. While ruling Italy, the French had introduced administrative reforms, many of which lasted beyond 1815. They also introduced, among certain classes, ideas of individual freedom and liberty.

Napoleonic France was defeated in 1815 by a coalition of the major European powers: the Austrian Empire, Britain, Prussia and Russia. After the Treaty of Vienna peace settlement of 1815, the Italian peninsula was dominated by a conservative Austria which intervened whenever necessary to prevent the spread of revolution; as in 1820–1 and 1831. However, the revolutionaries who were pushing for political change at this stage were not necessarily nationally minded but hoped for reform at a local level.

The *Risorgimento* is the name given to the process that ended with the political unification of Italy in 1871. It was primarily a cultural movement, aimed at spreading awareness of Italian culture and identity. However, there were significant political thinkers of the *Risorgimento*; most noticeably Giuseppe Mazzini. His belief in an Italy united as a democratic state was revolutionary for his time. Others put forward suggestions for a more conservative settlement; e.g. Vincenzo Gioberti argued in the 1840s for the creation of an Italian federation under the leadership of the Pope. Whatever their differences, all Italian intellectuals agreed that the Austrians should be expelled from Lombardy and Venice.

The Italian peninsula was wracked by the revolutions of 1848, as was most of Europe. In 1848 and 1849, attempts were made to expel the Austrians from the north of the Italian peninsula. These attempts failed and the lesson was learned that foreign military support would be necessary if such an action was to be successful. The following decade saw the emergence of Piedmont as the only Italian state capable of engineering such support. From 1848 to 1859, Austria dominated the Italian peninsula politically. Only with the decline in Austrian power and the emergence of France and Prussia was there an increased possibility for political change in Italy. Other foreign powers: Prussia, France, Britain and even (indirectly) Russia, had an important part to play in the process of Italian unification.

Under the leadership of its prime minister, Count Camillo Cavour, Piedmont became allied with France and, in 1859, fought a partially successful war of liberation from Austria. However, an accidental series of events and the intervention of one of the great heroes of the *Risorgimento*, Giuseppe Garibaldi, resulted in the near complete unification of Italy by 1861. Only Venice and Rome remained in foreign or papal hands. Again, circumstance intervened and events outside Italy contrived to result in the full unification of Italy as a nation state by 1870.

Risorgimento Translated,
the word means
'reawakening'. As a historical
term it has been used to
describe the development of a
national identity, a national
sentiment, an awareness
among Italians of a common
culture. It should not be used
to describe any movement for
national unification, because
there wasn't one.

**Victor Emmanuel II
(1820–78)** was the king of
Piedmont from 1849 to 1861
and first king of Italy from
1861 to his death in 1878. He
reigned as a constitutional
monarch, bound by the
Statuto which was granted by
his father Charles Albert in
1848. He made a number of
important decisions in his
reign, such as the appointment
of Count Camillo Cavour as
Prime Minister of Piedmont in
1852 or the decision to
support Garibaldi's expedition
in 1860.

**Massimo d'Azeglio
(1798–1866)** was an artist,
writer and, from 1849 to
1852, Prime Minister of
Piedmont. Unlike most
northern Italians, he travelled
to other parts of the
peninsula. However, he was
no different from most
northerners in his contempt
for the south. He commented
that the unification of the
north of Italy with the
Kingdom of Naples was like
'going to bed with someone
who has smallpox'.

CHAPTER 1

What was Italy like in the early nineteenth century?

INTRODUCTION

In September 1870, the troops of King **Victor Emmanuel II** of Italy entered Rome. Italian unification, the bringing together different states of the Italian peninsula under one government, was complete. The ***Risorgimento***, the reawakening of Italy, had reached its climax. However, the creation of the new Italian state was neither inevitable nor had it been planned. Although Italian unification had taken place, there was little enthusiasm for the new state among the Italian people. In 1861, an Italian politician named **Massimo d'Azeglio** remarked to Victor Emmanuel: 'Sir, we have made Italy. Now we must make Italians.' The story of what follows is of how Italy was made, but it is also a story of division and the failure to 'make Italians'.

WHAT WERE THE STATES OF THE PENINSULA?

Towards the end of the eighteenth century the peninsula of Italy was home to a number of states.

The Kingdom of Sardinia (Piedmont)

From its capital city of Turin, the **House of Savoy** ruled this relatively poor part of Italy. Despite its poverty, successive rulers built up a strong army and governed with an effective civil service. The island of Sardinia was particularly backward and was sparsely populated. Until 1815, the important port of Genoa was part of the Republic of Genoa. It was politically separate from the Kingdom of Sardinia.

Lombardy and Venetia

In the 1790s, Lombardy was part of the Austrian Empire. Its capital, Milan, was the second largest city of that empire. Lombardy was ruled by Austrian officials who acted in the name of the Austrian Emperor. However, they

were given a fair degree of freedom to act as they saw fit. The Austrian army underpinned imperial rule. It maintained a number of military strongholds known as the **Quadrilateral**, which dominated the plain of the fertile **Po Valley**.

ACTIVITY

Source A: Carlo Cattaneo was a writer from Lombardy. In the following extract from one of his books he is describing Lombardy in the 1840s.

The Lombard plain is the most populous region in Europe... Our rural municipalities have more schools...the poor are assisted at home by doctors...and the country is supplied with engineers. Landownership is common among all classes. All things considered this is the country with the largest number of educated families in proportion to the illiterate poor…no nation can compare with us for assiduous and preserving labour.

1. What impression does Cattaneo give of Lombardy in the 1840s?

2. What does this extract tell us about regional sentiment in Lombardy?

Republic of Venice

Otherwise known as the Republic of St Mark, this had been a powerful state in the fifteenth and sixteenth centuries because its merchants dominated trade in the Mediterranean. By the 1790s, the republic had lost its importance as a trading power, although not its architectural or artistic splendour.

The Central Duchies

This refers to the independent states of Tuscany, Modena and Parma. Tuscany had been governed by part of the Habsburg family, the House of Lorraine, since the 1730s. Relatively prosperous, Tuscany had been at the heart of the **Renaissance** from the fourteenth to sixteenth centuries. The city of Florence (the capital of Tuscany) became home to artists such as Leonardo da Vinci and Michelangelo. Modena and Parma were separated from Tuscany by the Apennine Mountains. These two states had a certain political independence – although, like Tuscany, they were within the sphere of Austrian influence.

The Kingdom of Naples

Ruled by the Bourbon family, the Kingdom of Naples was the poorest region of Italy. It was dominated by Naples, the largest city in Italy at the end of the eighteenth century with a population of 400,000. However, most of the population of Naples, and indeed the whole of the kingdom, lived in desperate poverty. In the countryside, the social structure and economic system was unchanged from medieval times. The land was owned by a few absentee landlords and the Church. The kings of Naples were absolute rulers who maintained large armies in order to control the people. '

ACTIVITY

Source A: Luigi Settembrini was a liberal who had been imprisoned by the Bourbon government in 1839 for alleged conspiracy. He was released from prison in 1842 but lost his job as a professor as a result of his imprisonment. However, he continued to conspire against the Bourbons. In 1847 he wrote the *Protest of the Peoples of the Two Sicilies* which was published anonymously. This is an extract from the book.

The foreigners who come to our country seeing the serene beauty of our sky and the fertility of our fields, reading the codes of our laws and hearing talk of progress, of civilisation and of religion, might believe that the Italians of the Two Sicilies enjoy an enviable happiness. And yet no state in Europe is in a worse condition than ours...in the country which is said to be the garden of Europe, the people die of hunger, are in a state worse than beasts.

Luigi Settembrini, from *Protest of the Peoples of the Two Sicilies*, 1847

1. What significance should be placed by the fact that Settembrini's book was published anonymously?

2. How far should we trust Settembrini's account?

WHAT WAS THE IMPACT OF THE FRENCH REVOLUTION, 1789?

The French Revolution of 1789 was to have a profound effect on Europe. Its impact on the development of Italy should not be underestimated. The revolution in France led to the absolute monarchy being swept away, and the introduction of political and administrative reform based, at least in theory, on the idea of liberty. Such ideas

**Napoleon Bonaparte
(1769–1821)** Became
Napoleon I, Emperor of
France from 1804–14 and
again in 1815. A brilliant
General, he also introduced a
number of administrative
reforms in France that have
lasted until today.

Papal States Stretching
from the cities of Ferrara and
Bologna in the north down to
Benevento in the south, the
Papal States dominated central
Italy. They were ruled by the
head of the Catholic Church,
who resided in Rome (for
centuries the centre of the
Catholic world). The Pope
was not just a spiritual leader,
he also had temporal power
(see Key Term on page 54). To
most Popes, control of the
Papal States was considered
essential to the protection of
papal independence. However,
the Popes did not have a
significant army and relied on
Catholic countries to protect
them militarily if required.

**Peace of Campo Formio,
1798** The Treaty of Campo
Formio ended Napoleon's
Italian campaign. Its main
significance was that the
Austrians recognised the
existence of the Cisalpine
Republic.

frightened the rulers of much of the rest of Europe. In
1792, Prussia and Austria launched into war on
revolutionary France. This affected Italy because of the
Austrian control of Lombardy and its considerable
influence over many of the other Italian states. As a result,
in May 1796, the young French General **Napoleon
Bonaparte** invaded northern Italy with the intention of
sweeping out the Austrians. A series of French victories left
Napoleon in control of most of northern Italy and from
1796 to 1799 he introduced a number of political changes:

- The regions of Lombardy, Modena, Bologna, Romagna
  and Ferrara were united into the Cisalpine Republic.
  This was administered on a model similar to that in
  France, with five directors and a legislature (Parliament).
  Unlike the French model however the legislature was
  appointed by Napoleon.
- The Republic of Genoa was transformed into the
  Republic of Liguria under French control.
- Until 1798, Piedmont was allowed to keep its monarchy,
  but lost Savoy and Nice to France. However, in 1799
  Piedmont was annexed to France.
- In 1796, the French had invaded the **Papal States**, but it
  wasn't until 1798 that they intervened in Rome and
  deposed the Pope, Pius VI. A revolutionary Roman
  Republic was set up under French control. The
  Republic's constitution was modelled on that of the
  French.
- In 1797, Napoleon invaded Venice but handed it over to
  the Austrians as part of the **Peace of Campo Formio** of
  October 1798 in return for territory in Belgium.

What was French interest and Italian reaction?

Some Italians, such as the *patrioti*, welcomed French rule.
The *patrioti* supported the attacks on Church privileges
and the destruction of old monarchies that took place after
1796. However, other Italians objected. In Naples in 1799,
a revolt against French rule ended in the slaughter of
thousands of middle-class supporters of the new order. In
December 1798, a coalition of anti-French states was
formed to push the French out of Italy. Known as the
Second Coalition, it planned for Russian and Austrian

armies to invade Italy. In April 1799, they invaded and defeated the French in a series of battles to the end of the year.

Despite this temporary setback for the French, it did not end their interest in Italy. Napoleon had been away in Egypt securing French control of parts of North Africa. On his return to France in late 1799, he seized political power by declaring himself First Consul and planned a new campaign in Italy. In May 1800, Napoleon led a large army across the Great St Bernard Pass and into northern Italy. He entered Milan, restored the Cisalpine Republic and moved rapidly to face a far larger Austrian army. At the Battle of Marengo on 14 June 1800, Napoleon won a great victory. This victory ensured French control of northern Italy for the next fourteen years. Again, the political map of the peninsula was redrawn.

- The Central Duchies were amalgamated in 1801 into the Kingdom of Etruria, which was eventually annexed to France.
- In 1805, the Cisalpine Republic became the Kingdom of Italy and Napoleon proclaimed himself its king. Napoleon chose as his viceroy his stepson, Eugene de Beauharnais. In the same year the north-west regions of Italy (including Piedmont, Parma and Liguria) were incorporated into France and ruled as French départements. The importance of this was that these regions were exposed to the administrative reforms introduced in France, known as the **Code Napoleon**.
- Between 1805 and 1808, Napoleon's armies took over different parts of the Papal States. Then, in 1809, Napoleon declared that Rome was to be the 'Second City of the Empire' that is, it would be incorporated into the French Empire. Pope Pius VII was to become a prisoner.

Napoleon was keen to give titles and land to as many of his relatives as he could. From 1806 the Kingdom of Naples was ruled by his brother Joseph, who became king. All feudal rights were abolished, a policy enforced by **Joachim Murat**. Sicily was not conquered by the French and was dominated by the British, who encouraged the introduction of a constitution in 1812 to be drawn up on British lines (in other words, there was a Parliament with two Houses and a constitutional monarchy).

WHAT WAS THE IMPACT OF NAPOLEONIC RULE IN ITALY?

Under French rule, many Italians experienced a transformation in how they were governed. Instead of a patchwork of customs and feudal laws that had dominated the running of so many of the states of Italy, they enjoyed the benefits of a new Code of Law. State officials administered parts of Italy under a unified and clearly defined system of rules. The Code forbade torture and stated that all people were equal in the eyes of the law. Even when the French were expelled from Italy and their laws repealed, it was difficult for the restored rulers to turn back the clock.

French rule sped up the process of the rise of the middle professional classes. In most regions of Italy before the 1790s, land was mainly owned by the aristocracy and the Church. However, Napoleonic rule meant the sale of large amounts of Church land. The peasantry did not benefit from this land sale because they could not afford to buy the land. Instead, the land was purchased by the commercial and professional middle classes. Indeed, many of the later leaders of the process of political unification such as **Count Camillo Cavour** came from families that made their fortunes in this period. Land sale also strengthened the position of members of the nobility, who were able to increase the size of their estates by buying Church land.

Popularity of French rule

The influence of the French revolution and the period of French dominance in Italy resulted in the emergence of secret societies. The societies were formed to plot against the French. When the French left Italy in 1814, they plotted against the restored governments. The stated aims of the largest society, the **Carbonari**, included the rejection

KEY PEOPLE

Count Camillo Cavour (1810–61) A Piedmontese statesman. He was prime minister from 1852 to 1859, during which time he modernised the economy. Cavour resigned as Prime Minister over the issue of the Treaty of Villafranca (see page 88).

KEY TERMS

The Carbonari The origins of this society are unclear, but translated the name means 'charcoal burners'. Every member of the society was sworn to secrecy in a special initiation ceremony. The Carbonari were committed to the principles of the rights of the people, and were prepared to use violence and revolution as the means by which it could achieve its aims. Although the Carbonari society was an international organisation, it was strongest in Naples where it had perhaps as many as 60,000 members.

of **absolutist government** and the protection of the rights of the people. After 1815, the secret societies were able to keep the idea of political reform alive even though change did not necessarily happen as a result of their activities.

However, French rule was by no means universally popular.

KEY TERMS

Absolutist government
This occurs when a ruler rules without constraints such as a Parliament.

- The demands of war had meant that taxation was high.
- Many Italians were conscripted into the army of the Kingdom of Italy, which, by 1810, was some 50,000 strong.
- Many Italians fought all over Europe for Napoleon and for the ideas that revolutionary France stood for. The idea that there should be a strong, secular (non-religious) centralised state would influence future generations of Italians.

Although demands for Italian unification were not strong in the opening years of the century, there had been a Kingdom of Italy, albeit one controlled from Paris.

The years of French dominance witnessed a serious attack on the Church as an institution. Although the Church was fully restored in 1815, the tradition of anti-clericalism was one that lingered.

WHAT WERE THE ECONOMIC ISSUES?

Land
The issue of land ownership was the foremost issue of the day. In *The Italian Risorgimento* (1998), Martin Clark argues that, throughout the nineteenth century, 'the real political issue was not constitutional liberty, nor independence, nor unification, but land'. As opportunities for investment in industry were so weak for much of the period in question, so land was the main form of investment. There was a significant difference in the patterns of land cultivation between the north and south.

KEY TERMS

Malaria An often fatal fever that is carried and passed on by mosquitoes.

- The soil in the south was inferior in quality and the region was crippled by **malaria**. Land was owned by absentee landlords and rented out by peasant farmers under a system known as the *latifundia*.

- Throughout the Italian peninsular and especially in the south, many were landless forced to work as labourers, but suffering from chronic underemployment.
- The period of Napoleonic rule had seen the abolition of feudal laws and the sale of Church land, which further encouraged land speculation. However, this did not result in a significant broadening of the range of people who owned land.
- In Piedmont and Lombardy there was more of a tradition of peasant landownership than elsewhere on the peninsula. In the middle of the century there were around 800,000 estates in Piedmont, although it should be stressed that many of these were small.

Industrial development

In no sense could Italy be described as being industrialised. There were signs of industrial development in certain regions, but the base of this development was narrow, being almost exclusively focused in textiles and light industry. There were a number of factors that hindered economic development in Italy and made any development there uneven.

- The Apennines, which form the physical spine of the country, acted as a barrier to transport communication between east and the west of the country.
- The political divisions made for localised rather than nationally based economies.
- In 1815 tariffs were re-imposed on trade between Italian states.

However, the period after 1815 saw the beginning of industrial growth. Most importantly, machines were imported from (primarily) Britain, France and Switzerland, which led to the creation of a factory-based textile industry. (In 1810, for example, the entrepreneur John Muller imported the machinery into Piedmont necessary for cotton manufacture.) However, there were factors that limited industrial growth, not least of which was that Italy relied on Britain for coal imports.

There was no sense in which the regions of northern Italy were integrated industrially. Indeed, because of Austrian domination of Lombardy and Venetia the regions' industries were in direct competition with those of its neighbours, notably Piedmont.

- The industrial economies were not broad enough, being concentrated in a number of urban centres such as Milan and with a limited range of industries, primarily cotton, wool and silk. The effect was that when there was a depression, the impact was considerable.
- Industry was still very much based at home and mostly linked to agricultural production.
- In the South there were few entrepreneurs with skills or capital to invest and few skilled workers. There was little natural source of power with which to run machinery.

HOW DID THE TREATY OF VIENNA AFFECT ITALY?

In 1815, the Napoleonic wars came to an end. The French Emperor Napoleon was banished to the island of St Helena in the Atlantic Ocean. Meanwhile, the victors of the war, Britain, Austria, Russia and Prussia, began to draw up a settlement that they hoped would ensure peace in Europe. The aim of the peacemakers was to return Europe to the days of political stability and to prevent France from ever causing such turmoil again.

One of the most influential peacemakers in 1815 was the Austrian foreign minister **Prince Klemens Metternich**. Indeed, he had considerable impact over Italian affairs for the next 30 years. In 1847, Prince Metternich commented that Italy was a mere 'geographical expression'. By this he meant that the idea of an Italian state was a fanciful one. For centuries the Italian peninsula was home to a number of distinct states with their own customs, governments, cultures and languages. In fact, the Italian language was only spoken by around 2.5 per cent of the population. The rest spoke in dialect.

The settlement of 1815, known as the Treaty of Vienna, reflected the diversity of Italy. Primarily, however, the Treaty reflected the wishes of Metternich and the ambitions

Liberals They believed that the best form of government was one that protected the people. Most liberals believed that this was best achieved through the creation of a Parliament that was elected by some of the people. They argued for a constitution that enshrined rights and liberties such as the freedom of speech. Liberals did not go as far as radicals who believed that all people should have the vote, that there should be far-reaching social reform and redistribution of power.

Nationalists They believed that nation states should be formed by people with a shared culture and identity. In Italy in 1815, there were few nationalists; most people identified with their locality such as Naples or Rome rather than their culture.

Victor Emmanuel I (1759–1824), King of Sardinia (1802–21) A conservative monarch, Victor Emmanuel was King of Piedmont from 1806 to 1821. For the first eight years of his reign, Piedmont was under the control of Napoleonic France, but Victor Emmanuel was restored to the throne in 1814. In March 1821, he was forced to abdicate in favour of his brother Charles Felix.

of Austria, which now had even greater control over Italian affairs. This would be a most important development. Many of the demands for political change in Italy after 1815 were not necessarily from a desire to unite Italy but rather from a desire to end Austrian control and influence.

In 1815, Metternich's wish was to restore the old pre-1796 order and this fact was reflected in the terms of the Vienna Settlement. He wished to impose a conservative settlement thereby crushing the hopes of **liberals** and **nationalists** across Europe.

The Treaty of Vienna had a considerable impact on the following states.

The Kingdom of Sardinia (Piedmont)

The Vienna treaty recognised the restoration of the House of Savoy as the rightful rulers of Piedmont. In 1814, **Victor Emmanuel I** returned to Piedmont and immediately began to restore the absolutist state. The Code Napoleon was repealed, as were various rights such as free and open trials. No laws passed after 1800 were recognised and the Church was restored to its pre-Napoleon privileged status. One important change introduced at Vienna was that the port and state of Genoa was granted to the House of Savoy.

Lombardy and Venice

Austrian dominance of Italian political life was assured by the return of Lombardy to Austrian control in 1814. However, it was strengthened by the recognition at Vienna of Austria's annexation of Venice.

The Papal States

By the terms of the Treaty of Vienna, Pope Pius VII was restored to his position as spiritual and temporal ruler of the Papal States. The Code Napoleon was abolished in most parts of the Papal States and the papal legal codes re-established. However, such a move was not universal. In Emilia-Romagna the Code Napoleon remained. Austrian influence over the region was considerably increased by the fact that Austrian armed forces were to be stationed in the Papal States. These forces were a sign that Austria would, if necessary, use force to protect the conservative settlement imposed on Italy.

The Central Duchies

The Treaty of Vienna left the Central Duchies firmly under Austrian influence. Grand Duke Ferdinand III, brother of the Austrian Emperor, became ruler of Tuscany. However, this did not mean that he was as conservative or as repressive as some of the other Restoration rulers. Indeed, Ferdinand and his first minister, Victor Fossombroni, improved education, set up hospitals and food relief during the outbreak of typhus in 1815–6, and allowed **freedom of expression**, which was not allowed in the rest of Italy.

The new ruler of Parma, **Marie Louise** of Bourbon-Parma, was equally broadminded. She scrapped the Code Napoleon in 1820, but replaced it with something similar. This was no surprise given the fact that she had been Napoleon's wife! In Modena, Duke Francis IV was far more repressive, reinstating the Jesuit order's influence over the lives of the Modenese.

The Kingdom of Naples

The Bourbon King, **Ferdinand I**, was restored to his throne in 1815 with vague promises of maintaining some of the legacy of French and British influence in Naples and Sicily respectively. However, this was not to be the case. The Church was restored to its position of power and authority. Many of the liberal projects introduced by the French such as road building and extending education were abandoned. In Sicily in 1816, the British-inspired constitution was destroyed; much to the frustration of many of the nobility who had enjoyed the power it had given them.

CONCLUSION

In 1815 although French rule had ended it did not appear that the regions which made up the Italian peninsula were moving closer to becoming a unified Italian state:

- The Vienna Settlement failed to wipe out all traces of Napoleonic rule in Italy.
- Austrian influence over Italy was considerable and Metternich's insistence that all traces of liberal government be suppressed was generally followed.
- There was little, if no, agitation for a form of united Italy. However, there were a number of Italians who hoped for an end to absolutist monarchy.
- The secret societies in particular were prepared to act in the name of change.
- There was significant economic disparity between the different regions of the Italian peninsular.

ACTIVITY

You have just read about the impact of the Treaty of Vienna on the Italian states. The following enquiry focuses on the nature of the settlement in 1815. There were a range of issues to be decided at Vienna including the role of Austria and the extent of the power given to the restored rulers.

The authors of the sources below come from very different backgrounds. Count Confalonieri was a liberal who had opposed Napoleonic rule but did not wish to see Austrian domination of the Italian peninsular. Cardinal Consalvi's interest was the power of the Papacy and that of the Church.

Enquiry
Study Sources A and B.

> Compare these Sources as evidence for the strength of desire to restore the Ancien Regime in the Italian states in 1815.

Source A: An appeal in 1814 by Milanese aristocrat and liberal Count Federico Confalonieri to British Foreign Minister Lord Castlereagh.

If our country has never enjoyed the advantages of political and national life, in the last twenty years it has learnt to desire them. We have intelligence, energy, passion, a wider experience

*of political matters and a greater love of our country and we
have learnt to fight. On the one hand, we are no longer the
same people who, twenty years ago were happy and lethargic
under the paternal rule of Austria; on the other, while I should
not like to be too bold in my assertion, I fear that perhaps the
Austrian government is no longer the same. Moreover, it will
not escape you that nature, language and customs limit all
countries and impose boundaries and special laws on them.
The history of the whole past century has shown how poorly
Austria has been able to protect our land.*

> From 'Rapporto dei deputati del regno d'Italia presso gli
> Allati'. In U. Foscolo, *Della sevitu dell'Itaial,* 1815

Source B: A report from Cardinal Ercole Consalvi to Pius
VII dated May 1815.

*Starting as always from his principle that we are being given
the Legations [Ferrara, Bologna, Romagna], not having them
restored to us, the Prince [Metternich] told me that Ferrara is
being given [to the Papacy] on condition that Austrian
garrisons should be stationed both there and at Comacchio. I
objected to this on the grounds that the Pope was an
independent sovereign but this objection was not considered
valid since Austria as donor is clearly allowed to attach rules to
her gift. We have decided to call these towns "frontier
fortresses".*

*The Prince also argued that the three provinces [of the
Legations]…accustomed for about twenty-five years now to a
system of government very different to Papal rule…could not be
brought under the old system of government. In my reply I
established that whatever the Holy Father was obliged to do in
the three Legations he would have to do in the rest of his
states. The Prince agreed, and so this was ruled out.*

> FS Orlandini, *Opera edite e postume*, vol. V, ed.
> Florence, 1850

CHAPTER 2

To what extent were the revolutions of 1820–1 and 1831 in the cause of national unity?

KEY ISSUES

All of Chapter 2 is important for evaluating **Key Issue 1** (see page iv).

KEY PEOPLE

Dante Alighieri (1265–1321) Born in Florence, he was an Italian poet. His importance to the story of the *Risorgimento* is that he defined the Italian language as it is used today.

Niccolò Machiavelli (1469–1527) The first great political philosopher of the Renaissance. His famous treatise, *The Prince* (written in 1513 and published in 1532), stands apart from all other political writings of the period in so far as it focuses on the practical problems a monarch faces in staying in power, rather than more speculative issues explaining the foundation of political authority.

KEY TERMS

Enlightenment This was a European movement which placed an emphasis on reason rather than tradition.

WHAT WAS THE *RISORGIMENTO*

The roots of an Italian national identity go back to the Roman Empire. During the Middle Ages, when Italy was divided politically into a number of small states, there were still those who thought in terms of Italy as a cultural identity at least. Most important of these was the writer **Dante**, who wrote in terms of Italia as a country. In the sixteenth century, one of the foremost Italian philosophers, **Niccolò Machiavelli**, wrote of Italia as a cultural entity. Neither wrote in terms of Italy as a nation state, because such an idea did not exist during their lifetimes. It was only in the late eighteenth and nineteenth centuries that awareness of national identity began to have political significance.

The term '*Risorgimento*' was first used in the context of national identity by S. Bettinelli in his cultural history of Italy entitled *Del Risorgimento d'Italia dopo il mille* (1775). In the same period, the writer Vittorio Alfieri wrote in terms of national identity.

ACTIVITY

Source A: From an extract from a book written by Alfieri in 1784.

*Of all of the enslaved countries in Europe, none is better suited to set up a new political system based on the ideas of the **Enlightenment** than Italy. This small peninsular is the same as that which previously conquered all of the then known world ... and which a few centuries later enlightened the rest of Europe with arts and sciences. The Italians possess a rather*

To what extent were the revolutions of 1820–1 and 1831 in the cause of national unity?

15

proud character and their sense of nobility leads me to believe and hope that they will be the first in Europe to set up an enlightened and politically stable society.

Adapted from Vittorio Alfieri,
Del Principe e delle Lettere, 1794

1. What features of Italy does Alfieri identify?

2. What does Alfieri hope and believe is Italy's destiny?

WHAT WERE THE FIRST REVOLUTIONS OF THE RISORGIMENTO?

The ideas of liberty were strengthened by revolution in France in the late 1780s and 1790s. This marks the beginning of a new phase of the *Risorgimento*, moving from a cultural-literary era to one in which political solutions were proposed. In France, **Jacobins** spoke in terms of justice, liberty and the brotherhood of man. Italian Jacobins were involved in plots to overthrow the government in Naples and Turin in 1794. Mainly educated people, they spoke in terms of liberty for the Italian people that could only be achieved with the destruction of autocracy. These were the first revolutions of the *Risorgimento* and the leading participants paid heavily with their lives, for example, in 1794, three leaders of the uprising in Naples (including 21 year-old Emanuele de Deo) were shot.

ACTIVITY

Italians varied in their political ambitions. Some hoped for nothing more than the abolition of **feudalism**. Others were more radical, hoping for a new Italy. The following extract was written by Melchiore Gioia. Originally ordained as a priest, Gioia was inspired by the French revolution to give up religious orders.

Source A: From an essay written for a competition sponsored by the pro-French administration of Lombardy which was set up in the wake of the successful French invasion of the region in 1796.

Jacobins The most ruthless radicals of the French revolution. They demanded universal liberty and, during **The Terror** of 1793–4, executed thousands of opponents.

The Terror is the name given to the period of French history between mid-1793 and July 1794. It is when the government, which was dominated by Robespierre, ordered the execution of thousands of its political opponents.

Feudalism A social and political structure based on land holding. At its heart was the idea of service to the lord, usually through military service, in return for land.

Federalism This is a system of government in which several states form a unity but retain independence in internal affairs.

*History shows us that Italy would be heading for disaster if she split up into small, isolated and independent republics. So let us look at the idea of federalism. Under such a system each region has its own political bodies, laws and interests which need to agree before anything is done so it is always slow to make plans. A **federal** Italy would be easy to invade as it would be difficult to get any of the states to agree to step forward to defend her. So I abandon this idea. Italy is open on all sides to foreign enemies, she needs the kind of government which will best be able to resist invasion. There is no doubt that this is a single indivisible republic.*

Adapted from Melchiorre Gioia, *Quale dei governi libri*, 1796

1. Explain Gioia's arguments for the future of Italy in your own words?

2. Why might the fact that Gioia has written this essay for a pro-French Lombard government have an impact on his proposals?

WHAT WERE THE SECRET SOCIETIES?

The period of French dominance in Italy was to lead to the development of secret societies such as the Carbonari and

'La Liberta insidiata dalla Tirannide' (Liberty resists the Tyranny).

To what extent were the revolutions of 1820–1 and 1831 in the cause of national unity?

the Adelfi whose members became disillusioned with, then actively opposed, French rule. The liberty that many Italians had hoped for did not materialise. The significance of groups such as the Carbonari was that they believed liberty could only be achieved with political change, either with the removal of the French or, after 1814, through revolution against the restored monarchies. Although the Carbonari were the largest secret society, there were others whose role in maintaining the revolutionary tradition should not be ignored. The Adelfi was a strongly anti-French society, which transformed itself into the strangely named Society of the Sublime Perfect Masters in 1818. Its main aim was the destruction of Austrian rule that would lead to a democratic republic. The leader of the Sublime Perfect Masters was **Filippo Buonarroti**, who was an experienced revolutionary. The society's membership was based in the north, which explains why the expulsion of Austria from Italian soil was considered the primary objective.

Although in the 1820s there were no national movements pressing for Italian unity, there were groups with serious grievances against the type of rule re-introduced after 1815. The types of people who joined the secret societies included those who had lost out from the restoration of old monarchies, including purged army officers and civil servants. These were more keen on radical action. Some wished for the restoration of lost political rights and **constitutions** that would guarantee those rights. A number of uprisings and revolutions in the 1820s and 1830s reflected dissatisfaction with a number of rulers. But this dissatisfaction often had causes related to local issues. The revolutions that took place were to challenge the legitimacy and rule of some of the restored rulers. However, they did not go so far as to challenge Austrian **hegemony**. Neither did they form the basis of a movement demanding change on a national basis.

ACTIVITY

One of the weaknesses of the Secret Societies were their often conflicting aims. Here are two extracts: Source A outlining the aims of the Carbonari, Source B the aims of the Society of the Sublime Perfect Masters. Both sources were issued around the end of the Napoleonic Wars.

Read through both sources and answer these questions:

- to what extent do the two sources differ?
- why the two sources differ?

Enquiry
Study Sources A and B

Compare these Sources as evidence for the aims of the Secret Societies.

Source A: Instructions of the Carbonari

Aims of the Order *The independence of Italy, our country. To give her a single, constitutional government, or at least to unite the various Italian governments in a confederation; all governments, however, shall be based on a constitution, freedom of the press and of worship, the same laws, currency and measures.*

Methods of the Order *To spread liberal ideas and communicate them to adherents, friends and clerics, by firmly convincing them of the unfortunate state of affairs in our Mother Country. The press, gatherings and private conversations are opportune means. Cunning and perseverance are needed and, above all, the eradication of all kinds of prejudice. The unprejudiced peasant is more enthusiastic than the rich man, the property owner, and is therefore more useful.*

Carte segrete e atti ufficiali della polizia austriace in Italia, vol I, Capolago, 1851

Source B: Profession of Faith of the Society of Sublime Perfect Masters

The divine origin of equality is sanctioned by the social contract. True liberty is to obey the general will of the people. Authority from any other source is to be condemned as evil.

The authority of law, whether exercised by a single person or by the many, can only be conferred by election. It can never be exercised for hereditary reasons or for life.

To what extent were the revolutions of 1820–1 and 1831 in the cause of national unity?

Anyone is permitted to kill a person who challenges supreme power.

Property boundaries shall be erased, all possessions shall be reduced to communal wealth, and the patria [the nation], shall provide food, education and work to all of her beloved and free children.

From A. Saitta, *Filippo Buonarroti*,
vol. I, Rome, 1950

WHAT WERE THE REVOLUTIONS OF 1820–1?

Naples

The restoration of the Bourbon monarchy in Naples was not without considerable problems. Ferdinand I and his chief minister Luigi de Medici introduced several measures that resulted in the most serious challenge to the restoration settlement to date.

- In 1818, Ferdinand restored the Church to a position of power and influence in Naples. Many Neapolitans were offended by the fact that the Church was given powers of censorship.
- The Bourbon monarchy was in financial difficulty after 1815. It had to pay for the Austrian army of occupation and reparations were imposed by Austria. The result of a heavy financial burden was cutbacks in government spending.
- During the British occupation of Sicily, the port of Palermo had flourished. However, a fall in agricultural prices had hit the port, as had the decline in trade.
- Union with Naples in 1815 was unpopular with many who disliked the absolutist Bourbons. The repeal of the Sicilian–British style constitution in 1816 was a source of considerable grievance for many. In both Naples and Sicily, liberals had hoped that the return of the Bourbons might bring with it a constitution that would guarantee political liberties.
- The trigger for revolution was the news from Spain of an uprising against King Ferdinand VII that had resulted in the promise of just such a constitution.

The Neapolitan revolt, 1820

In July 1820, an attempted revolution took place in Naples. However, the scale of the revolution was small: led by 30 members of the Carbonari supported by 100 soldiers from the local garrison. As the revolutionaries set out for the town of Avellino, their ranks were swelled by more members of the Carbonari rather than by peasants. The success of the uprising relied on the actions of an army officer, General Guglielmo Pepe, who led three regiments of soldiers in support of their cause (rather than against the revolutionaries). The result was that, on 6 July, King Ferdinand agreed to a new constitution. The next day, he clarified that this would be based on the **Spanish Constitution** model of **1812**.

So it seemed that the revolutionaries had succeeded. Pepe was put in charge of the army and a new government was sworn in that included a number of ministers from the Carbonari. However, the new government was quickly undermined by its own weaknesses. The Carbonari briefly won support as the rumours spread that it was on the verge of seizing Church property. But this was not the case. The Carbonari were divided among themselves and had no policies beyond the demand for a constitution.

Revolution in Sicily, 1821

Stories of the uprising in Naples spread to Sicily. There was considerable unrest in the capital Palermo. The cry went up in support of the introduction of a new constitution. The revolution was led by the workers of Palermo who belonged to the guilds of the city (known as the *maestranze*). There was little in their demands that suggested any nationalist sentiment. Indeed, the revolution was confined to Palermo and others in Sicily showed little sympathy for the cause of their revolutionary neighbours. Across the Straits of Messina, the new Neapolitan government also felt it necessary to restrain their revolutionary comrades, even if that meant using military force.

The events in the south of Italy did not go unnoticed in the rest of Europe. The revolutionary uprisings worried the Austrian foreign minister Prince Metternich to the extent

To what extent were the revolutions of 1820–1 and 1831 in the cause of national unity?

that he called an international congress at Troppau in October 1820 to discuss the issue. Metternich was the sworn enemy of revolutionary activity across Europe. **The Troppau Doctrine**, although agreed by the eastern powers, was not accepted by Britain.

In January 1821, Metternich called another Congress, this time at Laibach. He invited Ferdinand to attend, which he duly did. Once out of Naples, Ferdinand renounced the constitution and asked the Austrians for military support to crush his own government. In March 1821, Austrian troops entered Naples and the revolutionary government was crushed. Ferdinand unleashed a wave of **repression**, which saw a number of the Carbonari publicly executed. The importance of the Austrians as the ultimate arbitrators of Italian political life could clearly be seen.

Revolt in Piedmont, 1821

The diverse and localist nature of the secret societies such as the Carbonari can be seen by what happened next in Piedmont. In Naples, the Carbonari pushed for a constitution. In Piedmont, their demands were different in some ways. The restoration under Victor Emmanuel I had seen a return to autocratic and conservative monarchy. The Carbonari in Piedmont was made up of professional men and military officers who believed that the introduction of a **constitutional monarchy** would make possible their ultimate aim; the destruction of Austrian influence in Italy. The means by which such a change could take place was revolution. The revolutionaries pinned their hopes for a constitutional monarchy on the second in line to the throne, Charles Albert, Prince of Carignan.

The Neapolitan uprising of 1820 was an inspiration to a group of Piedmontese army officers who, in March 1821, seized the fortress of Alessandria and declared a provisional government. The revolution spread. In Turin, the army mutinied and Victor Emmanuel abdicated in favour of his brother, Charles Felix. The problem was that Charles Felix had left Piedmont on a visit to Modena. Therefore the next in line, **Charles Albert**, was appointed **regent**.

KEY TERMS

The Troppau Doctrine, 1820 Prussia, Austria and Russia agreed that it was the duty of the Great Powers to intervene militarily to support any government overthrown by revolution.

KEY THEMES

Repression Ferdinand I died in 1825, but his death did not end the repression. His successors Francis I and Ferdinand II continued to treat savagely all those who wanted political reform.

KEY TERMS

Constitutional monarchy The rule of a monarch who is bound in his or her actions to a constitution.

Regent Someone in temporary control.

KEY PEOPLE

Charles Albert (1798–1849) Second in line to the throne after Victor Emmanuel's brother Charles Felix, the young Prince Charles Albert was considered to be far more liberal in his views.

Some of the actions of the Piedmont rebels seem to point to the existence of a national sentiment, a desire for an Italian nation state.

- The revolutionaries declared that the king (Charles Albert) should be declared 'King of Italy'.
- Their demands were made 'in the name of the **Italian Federation**'.
- They were nationally minded in the fact that they wanted to expel the Austrians from Italy.

However, one should not exaggerate the extent of a national movement. The stress laid by the revolutionaries on the idea of Italy was mainly in response to the presence of Austria on Italian soil.

As regent, Charles Albert issued a constitution as demanded by the revolutionaries. However, on his return from Modena, Charles Felix was quick to reject any idea of a constitution. Indeed, he stated that he would not accept any change in 'the form of government' and promptly asked Metternich for military support. Charles Albert fled, recognising that the cause of political reform was a lost one. The revolutionaries under the command of Santorre di Satarosa raised an army, but it was defeated at Novara in April 1821 by a combination of Austrian and Piedmontese troops. Again, it was clear that Austria's domination was the most important factor in deciding the political fate of Italians. It was also clear that Piedmont was to be ruled in an autocratic manner by Charles Felix until his death in 1831.

WHAT WERE THE REVOLUTIONS OF 1831?

A number of Italian revolutionaries fled abroad after the failure of the 1820–1 uprisings. Many ended up in Paris and some even took part in the July Days uprising in France in 1830. The French king, Charles X, was overthrown by a mixture of **radicals**, **liberals** and the Paris mob. He was replaced by Louis Philippe, who promised to act as a constitutional monarch. To liberals in Italy, the revolution in France raised the possibility of French support for a similar revolution in Italy. Such support, in

To what extent were the revolutions of 1820–1 and 1831 in the cause of national unity?

their view, would act as a counter-balance to the power of conservative Austria.

Modena

The uprising in Modena was led by **Enrico Misley**. Misley's motivation for provoking revolution was primarily the achievement of Italian freedom from Austrian domination. He tried to enlist the support of the Duke of Modena, Francesco IV, by promising him support in becoming King of Italy. Initially, Francesco seemed interested. But he was acutely aware of the danger of challenging Austrian power.

Two days before the revolution was due to begin in February 1831, Francesco had Ciro Menotti, one of the important members of the conspiracy, arrested. However, revolution did go ahead in Bologna and quickly spread to Modena. Francesco fled to Vienna to plead for support from Metternich. While he was there, he heard news that the ruler of neighbouring Parma, Marie Louise, had fled in the face of similar demands for a constitution. However, revolutionary excitement did not last long. In March 1831, Francesco returned to the Central Duchies with an Austrian army and the revolutionaries were crushed. Many of the revolutionaries including Menotti were executed.

Revolution in the Papal States

Much more threatening to the established order in Italy was the outbreak of revolution in 1831 in the Papal States. Although not touched by the 1821 revolutions, there was repression of liberals and the secret societies were weaker than they were further south in Naples.

- In 1825, Leo XII was elected Pope. He immediately imposed a strict clerical regime.
- In 1829, Leo XII died. He was succeeded by Pius VIII.
- In 1830, Pius died after less than a year in office.

As revolution raged in the Grand Duchies, so its leader Menotti urged an uprising in the Papal States. A brief attempt at revolution by **Louis Napoleon Bonaparte** (Napoleon III) in Rome was a failure. However, a more serious reaction to clerical rule emerged. The aim of those who rose was not to create a united Italy, but to challenge the clerical state and to re-establish a secular state similar to that under Napoleonic rule. The aims of these revolutionaries in the Papal States in 1831 tells us much about the weakness of Italian nationalism in the period. Unlike Menotti, who had a vision of a revolution leading to the creation of some form of nation state, the revolutionaries in the Papal States wished for liberal reforms. It is accurate to describe their actions as those of revolutionaries. However, it is best to call this 'revolutionary liberalism' rather than 'nationalism'. The leaders of this moderate revolution were from the middle and artisan classes.

In February 1831, a revolutionary army led by Colonel Giuseppe Sercognani captured the papal port of Ancona and the Umbrian capital Perugia. In March 1831, a provisional government led by the elderly Giovanni Vicini was set up in Bologna. In March 1831, it issued a constitution promising the following:

- A reformed finance system with moderated tariffs.
- An elected assembly that would choose a president and cabinet.
- A fairer judicial system based on the Napoleonic model.

This constitution was not particularly radical, but it was too much for the Austrians. For Metternich, revolutionary liberalism was as much a threat to the established order as revolutionary nationalism.

KEY PLACES

The Marches is the region in the east of central Italy. It stretches from the Apennine Mountains to the Adriatic Sea.

In March 1831, an Austrian army intervened and took Bologna with relative ease. The revolutionary army surrendered to papal forces believing the papal intermediary Cardinal Benvenuti when he promised an amnesty for all those who had taken up arms against papal rule. They were mistaken to trust Benvenuti. Papal armies swept through the **Marches** acting in a manner that was to sow the seeds for further revolution.

ACTIVITY

Use the information in Source E and your own knowledge to answer the following question.

To what extent were the revolutions of 1820–1 and 1831 in the cause of national unity?

1. What was the extent of Austrian power in Italy in the
   years from 1815 to 1831?

Source A: This is an extract from a book by the historian
Martin Clark.

*These revolts showed that Restoration regimes were vulnerable.
The real danger came from palace coups, from officers in the
elite army corps ... [who were] strongly influenced by heroic
risings abroad. However, the Austrians would soon restore the
previous regime. Restoration governments had few reliable
troops of their own; but they did have the Austrian army
available in time of need. This was a trump card.*

From Martin Clark, *The Italian Risorgimento*, 1998

CONCLUSION

With hindsight one should judge that the revolutions of
1831 were a hopeless cause. They failed for a number of
reasons:

- They did not constitute a national uprising, but were
  regionally based revolts.
- There was little, if any, communication of support from
  revolutionaries in one region such as Bologna for those
  in another such as Modena. This was partly because the
  ambitions of the revolutionaries were limited by their
  localism.
- The social base of the revolutionaries was narrow. As
  already noted earlier, Misley was an academic, Menotti a
  prosperous businessman. The revolutionaries of 1831 did
  not have a broad popular support. Often they were
  members of exclusive secret societies such as the
  Carbonari. Because of their social background, the
  revolutionaries were not attempting a social revolution.
  In most cases their aims were constitutional, to extend
  power to their class through the granting of a
  constitution.
- Most importantly, the revolutionaries of 1831 failed to
  attract foreign support to counteract the impact of
  Austria. Misley had hoped for support from the

**Louis Philippe
(1773–1850)** Born in Paris,
he became known as the
'Citizen King'. He reigned
from 1830 to 1848. In 1848,
when the Paris mob rose he
abdicated and fled to England.

KEY THEMES

**Policy of non-
intervention** In 1831, Louis
Philippe's minister Casimir
Perrier stated: 'We do not
recognise the right of any
people to force us to fight in
its cause; the blood of
Frenchmen belongs to France
alone.'

government of the French King **Louis Philippe**, who
had only recently been brought to power by a similar
type of liberal revolution. However, Louis Philippe
quickly dashed the hopes of the revolutionaries by
stating clearly that it was not the responsibility of the
French to interfere in other countries' affairs. The
problem was that this **policy of non-intervention** was
also adopted by those in one part of Italy who identified
themselves through their region and argued that it was
not in their interests to fight for the cause of other
Italians in other parts of the country. Without the
support of a foreign power the revolutionaries had little
chance of standing up to the might of the Austrians.

To what extent were the revolutions of 1820–1 and 1831 in the cause of
national unity?

CHAPTER 3

How did the *Risorgimento* develop from 1830 to 1847?

INTRODUCTION

There are many important issues addressed in this chapter. Perhaps the most important are the ideas raised, and the role played in the *Risorgimento* by Giuseppe Mazzini. The other important issue is the extent and impact of the *Risorgimento* in Italy in the years from 1830 to1847.

YOUNG ITALY

It was the failure of the secret societies in the 1820s and 1830s revolutions that led to the founding of a new organisation, **Young Italy**, by **Giuseppe Mazzini** in 1831. This new organisation did not reject all aspects of the secret societies. It looked after its members, and gave them passwords, uniforms and ritual. However, there were differences in both organisation and philosophy that were to make Young Italy distinct.

The organisation was accompanied by a journal edited by Mazzini, also entitled *Young Italy*. This journal was important in spreading Mazzinian ideas:

- At the heart of Mazzini's ideas was a belief in democracy and that the will of the people, *la plebe*, should be listened to. In his view, God's Will was expressed through the people and therefore their demands mirrored the demands of the Lord.
- In Mazzini's view, the will of the people was to live in an independent nation of 'free men and equals'. To achieve this independent nation it was necessary to engage in a national revolution.
- Where Mazzini differed was in the breadth of his vision. He did not just see a union of northern Italian states, as did so many other patriots. He envisaged a union of all

KEY ISSUES

The events of this chapter are important in evaluating **Key Issue 1** (see page iv).

KEY TERMS

Young Italy Founded in 1831, this organisation had an impact on the political development of Italy. The uniform of Young Italy was somewhat theatrical, which was in keeping with much of what Mazzini did. The national colours of Italy were worn in combination with a green blouse being complemented with a red belt and white trousers.

KEY PEOPLE

Giuseppe Mazzini (1805–72) Born in Genoa, Mazzini's training as a lawyer came a distant second in importance to his career as a revolutionary nationalist. Indeed he was bored by the study of law and quickly became interested in politics. He joined the Carbonari in 1827, but became disillusioned with its secrecy and the lack of debate among members about the future of Italy. Indeed, Mazzini was eventually betrayed to the authorities in Genoa by a fellow member of the Carbonari, Raimondo Doria. While in prison in 1830, Mazzini came up with the idea of Young Italy.

Giuseppe Mazzini, the founder of Young Italy.

Italian-speaking provinces – including the south, Sicily and Sardinia. In 1829, he clearly summarised his vision: 'The fatherland of an Italian is not Rome, Florence or Milan but the whole of Italy.'

- Young Italy was republican in its views. This did not mean that Mazzini dismissed out of hand constitutional monarchies. These were, in his view, useful as a stepping stone – 'governments of transition' – on the way to the ideal: a united Italian republic. Indeed, in 1831 Mazzini wrote to the King of Piedmont, Charles Albert, asking him to put himself at the head of the movement for a united Italy. In his letter, Mazzini asked that the king lead the nation and put on his banner 'Union, Liberty, Independence'.

ACTIVITY

Source A: The means by which Mazzini's aims were to be achieved are expressed in the following extract from a *Young Italy* manifesto written by him in 1831.

The means of fulfilling the aims of Young Italy are education and insurrection (uprising). These two methods must be made to work in agreement and harmony. Education, by writing, example and word, must always preach the necessity of insurrection, and when it succeeds must provide a principle of national education.

Italy can free herself by her own strength. To successfully found a nation it is necessary to be conscious of nationality and this consciousness cannot be obtained if insurrection is achieved or triumphs through foreign hands.

Adapted from a *Young Italy* manifesto, 1831

1. What are the means by which Mazzini believes the Italian nation can be built?

2. Given the events of the revolutions in the 1820s and early 1830s, why might Mazzini's plans be considered as flawed?

The failures of Young Italy

The ideas of Young Italy were spread from Marseilles in France (Mazzini's base) to Piedmont, the Papal States and Tuscany. In Piedmont, the readership of Young Italy grew and new adherents to the cause of revolution were recruited. However, the attempts at revolution ended in farce.

- In 1833, a proposed army coup was detected before it could begin. The response of Charles Albert's government was ferocious. Twelve members of Young Italy were executed out of 67 people arrested.
- In 1834, a planned attack on Piedmont fizzled out before it started. An uprising in Genoa scheduled for February 1834 and led by a new recruit to the Young Italy movement, **Giuseppe Garibaldi**, also failed to get off the ground.

WHAT WAS THE IMPACT OF MAZZINI?

Mazzini lived in Switzerland and London from 1834 to 1849. Although his attempts at revolution in the 1830s seemed to be feeble and unrealistic, his ideas, were an

KEY ISSUES

Mazzini is one of the individuals listed in **Key Issue 3** (see page iv). How much of an influence and contribution did his actions and ideas make to Italian unification?

KEY PEOPLE

Giuseppe Garibaldi (1807–82) Garibaldi was the most famous soldier and patriot of the *Risorgimento*. Born in Nice, he became a follower of Mazzini and had to flee Italy in the 1830s. He went to South America where he became involved in a number of wars. He returned to Italy in 1848 and, although a republican, joined with Charles Albert of Piedmont in his attempt to free Italy of Austrian rule. He led the army of the ill-fated Roman Republic in 1849 and after its collapse he fled to the United States of America. In 1860, he played an important part in the unification of Italy by conquering the Kingdom of the Two Sicilies with his army of soldiers known as the Red Shirts. He was involved in two attempts to take Rome by force in the 1860s and in 1874 was elected to the Italian Parliament. He was the hero of his day.

inspiration to others. Giuseppe Mazzini and the revolutionary ideal for Italian rebirth that he promoted were of critical importance in providing a model for change and in fostering a national consciousness.

Mazzini and democracy

Mazzini believed that nation states should be based on the principle of democracy, thereby making them fully representative of the people who lived in, and belonged to, those states. Yet although Mazzini proposed democracy and wished to see the nation state built by 'the people', in reality his views were shared by a small minority. Many of those who took part in the Mazzinian-inspired revolutions of 1821 or 1831, or those such as the **Bandera brothers** (whose gallant but flawed invasion of Calabria in 1844 led to their martyrdom) were from privileged backgrounds.

At no time between 1830 and 1870 was the peasantry willing to support a Mazzinian-inspired uprising. This was because Young Italy did little by way of proposing a solution to the deep social and economic poverty of many of those living in the Italian states. The most important issue for the peasantry across the Italian peninsular was not the creation of a nation state but land ownership, the enclosure of land and the ending of feudal common land rights. These had been undertaken by the middle class who were demanding political rights to complement their economic power. There was, therefore, little common ground between Mazzinian nationalists and the peasantry.

HOW DID NATIONAL IDENTITY DEVELOP?

Language divisions

In *Italy: A Modern History* (1959), the historian Denis Mack Smith made the point that even individuals who had an important impact on the development of Italian politics including Garibaldi and Cavour had 'an imperfect knowledge of the Italian language'. The latter, in particular, preferred to converse in French. At first it seems ironic that two of the leading characters of the story of Italian unification were not fluent in Italian. However, there was no native Italian tongue. The Italian peninsula was a

KEY PEOPLE

Attilio and Emilio Bandera Officers in the Austrian Navy. They eventually deserted and launched an invasion of Calabria in 1844. The problem was that there were only nineteen of them and their numbers had swelled by two by the time the authorities arrived. The Bandera brothers were shot, but in their death they became important martyrs for the cause of national unity.

KEY ISSUES

Garibaldi is one of the individuals listed in **Key Issue 3** (see page iv).

patchwork of languages and regional dialects. The Italian language as we know it came from the Tuscan dialect and was only spoken in Florence. Indeed, even as late as 1871, it is likely that it was only known and commonly used by around 630,000 out of a population of nearly 27 million.

Such linguistic diversity was at the heart of Metternich's dismissal of Italy as a 'mere geographical expression' in 1815 and D'Azeglio's concern that the first priority of the rulers of the new state in 1861 was to 'make Italians'.

ACTIVITY

Source A: Alessandro Manzoni, one of the most famous Italian writers of the nineteenth century, explains some of the issues surrounding language.

There is no uniformity of language in Italian literature. If there were then we would not have to deal with the task of creating a common tongue. All over Italy there is a common spoken language of a kind. However, most people including the well-to-do speak in dialect. Imagine a group of Milanese [from Milan] are talking in dialect as would be the normal custom throughout Italy. Introduce into this circle people from Piedmont, Bologna, Venice and Naples and watch them try to talk in Italian. They will probably have to use more general terms but when speaking in dialect they had a precise one? In desperation they might use words which are not Italian or they might try to Italianise a Milanese word. Is this really to posses a language in common?

Adapted from notes written by Alessandro Manzoni, 1836

1. What does Manzoni identify as the problems of language in Italy?

2. How representative is Manzoni of opinion in the first half of the nineteenth century?

Despite the dominance of dialect, there was progress towards a national language.

- In Tuscany, the ideas of national identity were spread in the pages of the journal *Antologia* (see Key Term on page 12).
- In Lombardy, there were those who encouraged the use of Italian as part of their expression of national identity. The Italian language periodical *Biblioteca Italiana* was founded in Milan in 1816 and the journal *Il Politecnico*, which was produced in Milan between 1839 and 1845. Such journals raised consciousness of a common culture and language among the educated classes.

Equally important in the development of an Italian national consciousness was the creation of national rather than regional organisations, such as the *Congresso degli Scienziata* (Congress of Science) which met in different parts of Italy between 1839 and 1847. These meetings were attended by delegates from many different regions. The topics discussed were wide ranging, from the latest medical research to agricultural innovation. The language used at the meetings was Italian and there was a political edge to their agenda. At a *Congresso* meeting held in Genoa in 1846, the occasion was used to celebrate the victory of Italian arms over the Austrians in 1746. Many of the future heroes of the *Risorgimento* attended the *Congresso*. They provided a function as a nursery for more moderate (in comparison to Mazzinian) nationalist opinion.

WHAT WERE THE PATRIOTIC THEMES IN MUSICAL AND LITERARY WORKS?

In the 1840s, the *Risorgimento* was marked by the increase in the number of cultural works with patriotic themes.

Music

The most famous Italian operatic composer was **Giuseppe Verdi**. In the work he composed in the 1840s there were clear political messages.

- The opera *Nabucco* (first performed in 1842 in Milan) included the famous stirring 'Chorus of the Hebrew Slaves'. The parallel to be drawn between the enslavement of the Israelites and the repression of the Italians was clear for many in the audience.

- Equally nationalistic was the opera *I Lombardi*, first performed in 1843.

The performance of Verdi's works became linked with anti-Austrian sentiment. Such was the impact of Verdi on nationalist opinion that, at times of tension, performances of his work caused outbursts of violence between Italian patriots and Austrian army officers. The operas of Verdi in the early 1840s especially inspired the Milanese nationalist middle class. The 'Chorus of the Hebrew Slaves' in *Nabucco* (1842) was written to represent the enslavement of the Italian peoples. But Verdi's interpretation was not typical of the view of the majority of those who lived on the Italian peninsula and even those who lived in Lombardy.

Literary works

Throughout the 1840s, a number of literary works helped to define even further the Italian national identity and provoke debate among nationally minded Italians about the future of the country. The Mazzinians still hoped for a unitary state brought about by revolution, but many more 'moderate' Italians believed that the way forward was for a federation of Italian states. The roots of these federal ideas was the fact that economic growth in Lombardy and other areas had meant that significant numbers of middle-class Italians saw closer economic ties between the Italian regions as progress.

Vincenzo Gioberti

For much of the middle part of the nineteenth century, the Pope was assumed to be the natural leader of any federal Italian state. Highly influential in the development of this line of thought was **Vincenzo Gioberti**. The publication in 1843 of *Primato Morale e Civile degli Italiani* ('On the Moral and Civil Primacy of the Italians') was to have widespread consequences.

- Gioberti agreed with Mazzini that Italy should be rid of foreign influence, both French and Austrian. However, he thought Mazzini was mad and his tactics damaging. Instead, in *Primato* Gioberti outlined a more moderate approach to ensuring Italian liberty.

- In the book, Gioberti argued in favour of Italian independence; the creation of an Italian federation under the leadership of the Pope.
- He argued that the Italian states should be drawn together in a federation under the leadership of the Pope. He believed that it was the papacy in Rome that gave Italians the moral upper hand over other European peoples.
- This line of thought became known as **neo-Guelph**. It appealed to many as it offered a way forward without revolution. It particularly appealed to those who disliked the idea of a French-style unitary state as suggested by Mazzini and his followers.
- The weakness of Gioberti's book was that it failed to mention the issue of Austrian control of Lombardy or Venetia and the fact that papal rule of the Papal States had not exactly been popular or effective.

Gioberti's views appealed to Italian Catholics but were not universally popular. A group of Italian writers, including Giuseppe La Farina, attacked the idea of extending papal power. However, the most important legacy of the *Primato* was to spread the idea of a papal-led resolution to the national question. This was to have an important effect on a priest named Giovanni Maria Mastai-Feretti who, in 1846, was elected as Pope Pius IX. However, it was not just Gioberti who asserted the primacy of the Pope. Further evidence can be seen at Plombières in 1859, when Napoleon insisted that the Italian federation he envisaged would be led by Pius IX. This was not just Napoleon trying to please the Catholics in France. The papacy's spiritual position as the leader of the world's foremost faith, and the importance of Catholic opinion in France, Austria and parts of Germany, made the Pope seem the natural leader. One should also remember that the Pope ruled over a considerable part of central Italy as a feudal lord.

Cesare Balbo

Gioberti's ideas had a strong influence on **Count Cesare Balbo** whose book, *Le Speranze d'Italia* ('The Hopes of Italy') was published in 1844. Balbo predicted many of the diplomatic and political developments of the coming years.

- Like Gioberti, Balbo argued in favour of a federation of states. However, his view of Italy was limited to the north.
- While accepting the importance of the papacy, Balbo suggested that the Piedmontese monarchy should take the lead in expelling the Austrians from Lombardy and Venice.
- Most significantly, Balbo argued that the solutions to the dilemmas facing Italian nationalists would not be found in revolution but through Italian and European diplomacy. Balbo felt that if **Austria** were to be pushed out of Italy, it could look east to **the Balkans** for territory and influence. This was to be a prophetic suggestion.
- Balbo failed to address in *Le Speranze* the issue of what would happen when the Austrians decided they did not want to move out of Lombardy. This fact did not prevent his book becoming very popular in Piedmont and especially at the court of the Piedmontese king, Charles Albert.

ACTIVITY

Enquiry
Study Sources A and B.

Compare these Sources as evidence for proposals for Italy's future.

Source A

I intend to prove that, mainly because of religion, Italy possesses within herself all of the necessary conditions for her national and political rebirth, and that to achieve this in practice she has no need of internal revolutions, nor of foreign invasions or imitations. And in the first place I say that before all else Italy must resurrect her life as a nation; and that national life cannot exist without political union between her various parts… That the Pope is naturally and must in practice be the civil head of Italy is a truth proven by the nature of things, confirmed by the history of many centuries, recognised on occasions by our people and princes.

Vincenzo Gioberti, *Primato,
Morale e Civile degli Italiani*, 1843

Austria and the Balkans
In 1866, Austria handed Venice over to the new Italian state after its defeat by the Prussians in the Austro-Prussian war. Although it was to hold on to Italian land (known as the irredentist lands) in the north such as Trent and Trieste, Austria did turn its attention to the Balkans for influence – for example, in 1908 it annexed Bosnia Herzogovina.

Source B

No nation has been less frequently united in a single body than the Italian... The dreamers say that one can still achieve what hitherto has never been achieved... What would be the pope's position in a kingdom of Italy? That of king? But this is impossible, nobody even dreams of it. That of subject? But in that case he would be dependent. A democratic system may continue to be, for some time, the fear of the police and the hope of secret societies but it cannot enter into any assessment of the foreseeable future.

The worthy House of Savoy has upheld the sacred fire of Italian virtue for the last century and a half. All states that have come under their control have been in favour of the monarchy of Savoy and have been acquired at the expense of the House of Austria; for the most part by fighting for them.

Cesare Balbo, *Le Speranze d'Italia,* 1844

Massimo d'Azeglio

Another important intellectual whose work strengthened the argument for more conservative political change was Massimo d'Azeglio. In September 1845, D'Azeglio was to witness first hand an attempted revolution in Romagna in the Papal States. The following year he published his account of the revolution in *Degli Ultimi Casi di Romagna* ('On Recent Events in Romagna'). D'Azeglio was very clear in his conclusions.

- Those that had died in the Romagna revolution should be treated as martyrs, because they had fought against Austrian and Papal tyranny.
- However, he argued that revolution was not the way forward.
- Balbo and **D'Azeglio** agreed that **public opinion** and European opinion were crucial. If it was well informed and positive, then change would come about naturally.

The significance of Balbo's and D'Azeglio's books is that they argued that liberation of the Italian peoples could and should come from above and should result in a far more conservative settlement than suggested by Mazzini.

Therefore, they represent a very significant development in the *Risorgimento*. No longer should it be dominated by the tactic of popular uprising. The debate was now open to the possibility of political change engineered from above. Such a blueprint was to attract the interest of Pius IX for at least a few years and, later, Count Cavour.

WHO SUPPORTED THE *RISORGIMENTO*

The relationship between the middle class and the aristocracy has caused some historical debate. In *The Italian Risorgimento* (1998), Martin Clark argued that the migration of many aristocrats to urban areas led to a fusion of interests between them and the middle class. To Clark this is a critical point as 'it is the key to understanding the *Risorgimento*. It created an effective new elite, used to acting together and less beholden to the existing states.' This viewpoint is countered in *Italy: A Modern History* (1959) by Denis Mack Smith, who saw the decline in the nobility as leading to friction with the emerging middle class that sought economic and political power. He wrote that 'the *Risorgimento* was a civil war between the old and new ruling class'. Evidence can be found to support both interpretations often depending on the region studied:

- in Sicily the nobility remained aloof and declined the opportunity to modernise.
- in Tuscany there was a greater fusion of interest between nobility and the middle class.

The extent of division between nobility and middle class often helps explain the nature of the course of the *Risorgimento* in various regions.

The greatest cultural division in Italy was between the wealthier classes and the mass of the poor. For most of those living on the Italian peninsula, the question of the day was not the political shape of Italy or of constitutions but of daily survival. The threat to that survival came from a number of sources. Add to this the diversity of language and culture, and the lack of communication and education, and one can understand why the peasantry and urban workforce were invariably the classes that resisted any political change that might make their plight worse.

CONCLUSIONS

By the mid-1840s, the ideas of national identity had began to move towards ideas of national unity. There were common themes among Italian patriots, most obviously the desire to destroy Austrian influence and interference in Italy. However, there were different strands of thought about how this might take place. Most important were:

- Mazzinian ideas of revolution leading to a unitary Italian state, preferably a republic.
- Moderate opinion in favour of a more gradual approach resulting in constitutional government.
- Neo-Guelph ideas of a federal state under the direction of the papacy.

There was considerable social and cultural division in Italy throughout the first half of the century.

However, the events of 1848–9 were to decide the most likely means by which change would take place.

CHAPTER 4

How significant were the revolutions of 1848–9?

KEY ISSUES

This whole chapter is devoted to the events and analysis of **Key Issue 2** (see page iv).

KEY PEOPLE

Pius IX (1792–1878) Pope from 1846 to 1878, Pius IX was one of the most influential figures of the *Risorgimento*. His parents wanted him to have a career in the military, but his health was not deemed sufficiently robust. Instead he became a priest and a cardinal in 1839.

INTRODUCTION

There were many causes of the revolutions that spread across Italy and beyond during 1848–9. The hopes and expectations of liberals for reform were heightened by the election of **Pius IX** in 1846. Added to this was the clamour of nationalists for the destruction of Austrian power, which increased as the Austrian Empire seemingly faltered. Agitation was increased by the economic crisis that swept Europe in 1846–7 as a result of harvest failure in 1846. For eighteen months the Italian peninsula was in turmoil until the gains won by liberals were reversed and the revolutions that had taken place were suppressed.

WHAT WERE THE CAUSES OF THE 1848 REVOLUTIONS?

The reforms of Pope Pius IX

In 1846, Pope Gregory XVI died. He was succeeded by Cardinal Mastai Ferretti, who chose the title Pius IX. Immediately, Pius extended a hand of reconciliation to the liberals by declaring an amnesty for political offences, releasing some 2,000 prisoners from papal gaols. Such a move impressed the liberals, as did Pius' appointment of the liberal Cardinal Gizzi as his Secretary of State. A number of reforms followed:

- In 1847, press censorship by the Church was ended and censorship in the Papal States was undertaken by a committee of predominantly laymen. This move allowed the creation of a freer press in the Papal States that was to have important consequences later on.
- A civic guard of local people was created to protect property. The guard was armed. The guard quickly gained members who were sympathisers of Mazzinian demands for a republic.

- A Council of State, the Consulta, was set up in 1847 to advise the papacy on how to run the Papal States. Although its powers were limited, to many liberals it was the first step on the road to the elected Parliament they so desired.

The motivation of Pius IX in allowing these reforms was to make papal rule more effective and popular (although the former criteria was by far and away the most important). However, in doing so he appeared to be a 'liberal pope', something that Metternich in particular found very worrying.

ACTIVITY

The following source reveals some of Metternich's concerns. Read the source through carefully.

Source A: Written by Metternich to Austrian agents in Milan and Paris.

Each day the Pope shows himself more lacking in any practical sense. Born and brought up in a liberal family, he has been formed in a bad school; a good priest he has never turned his mind towards matters of government. Warm of heart and weak of intellect he has allowed himself to be taken and ensnared in a net from which he no longer knows how to disentangle himself, and if matters follow their course he will be driven out of Rome. A liberal Pope is not a possibility.

Adapted from letters by Metternich, October and December 1847

1. What are Metternich's criticisms of Pius IX?

2. How reliable is this letter in describing Metternich's true thoughts about Pius IX?

Under the Treaty of Vienna the Austrians were given the right to keep an army in the town of Ferrara, despite the fact that it was inside the Papal States. In July 1847, the city was occupied by Austrian troops. Pius IX responded in a way that raised his reputation with Italian nationalists to even greater heights.

- He lodged a formal protest with the Austrian government claiming that the sovereignty of the Papal States had been infringed.
- He proposed a customs union of Italian states in which trade could take place without tariffs (taxes) being imposed. A treaty was signed in November 1847 with Tuscany and Piedmont, but which left out the states controlled by Austria.

The impact of Pius IX's reforms in other parts of Italy was considerable. In Piedmont there was unrest and demands for change. The response of Charles Albert in Piedmont in October 1847 was to sack his conservative minister, Solara della Margarita, and announce a package of limited reforms. He allowed press censorship to be relaxed and local government was reorganised. As is often the case, granting reform did little to satisfy liberals and radicals who simply increased their **demands for reform**. The same applied to Tuscany where Duke Leopold II introduced limited reforms that only served to encourage radicals to demand a constitution.

Economic problems

Agitation for political reform was partly the result of economic problems in Italy during 1846–7. In particular, the poor harvest led to food riots from north to south and made deep-rooted economic problems worse.

- In southern areas such as Calabria, land enclosure had taken **common land** from the peasantry. Their response was violence.
- In the north, under-employment in the textile industries resulted in workers destroying machinery.

So the initial cause of unrest was social. But the unrest soon turned into a political demonstration, stirred by a free press.

WHAT HAPPENED IN SICILY?

KEY TERMS

Cholera A very infectious disease, often fatal. It is caused by poor sanitation and infected water supplies.

KEY EVENTS

Uprising in Palermo: January 1848 The initial manifesto called Sicilians to rally 'to arms, sons of Sicily; our united force will be invincible'. Unfortunately it didn't mention where they might get these arms.

KEY THEMES

Sicilian elections The elections to the Sicilian Parliament were open to all literate males in Sicily at the time. This did not constitute a large proportion of the population.

KEY TERMS

'King Bomba' Translated from Italian, *bomba* literally means 'bomb'.

The uprising in Sicily in 1848 was not caused by any demands for national unity. Instead, it was a reaction against the repressive regime of Ferdinand II. In 1836, an outbreak of **cholera** on the island killed one-tenth of the Sicilian population (some 65,000 people) and led to the belief that the disease was in some way connected to Neapolitan misrule. A lack of political debate, a police state and miserable living conditions provoked an **uprising in Palermo** on 12 January 1848. After a few days, the revolutionaries had taken control of the city and the revolution was being led by Sicilian nobleman Rosalino Pilo. The main demand of the revolutionaries was straightforward. They wanted the re-establishment of the 1812 constitution, which had been abolished by the King of Naples in 1816. Ferdinand II would not accept the reintroduction of such a constitution, because it would have given Sicily considerable autonomy from Naples. He offered a compromise constitution, which was refused. The Sicilian revolutionaries consequently set up their own provisional government. The nature of this government reveals much about the nature of the revolution.

- A National Guard was established to ensure that the lower orders and the more militant revolutionaries did not get out of control.
- Hostility was maintained towards Naples and all key government posts were reserved for Sicilians. The **Sicilian elections** took place in March 1848. In April 1848, the newly elected Parliament announced that Ferdinand was no longer King of Sicily. An Italian prince would be chosen as monarch in his place.
- In July 1848, the Sicilian constitution gave considerable powers to the lower house of Parliament.

This was not a radical revolution, but one that aimed at a constitutional settlement that would give Sicily its independence. However, this was not acceptable to Ferdinand and, in September 1848, he launched a military assault on the island, which earned him the nickname **'King Bomba'**. Despite the superiority in numbers of the

Neapolitan army, it took them until May 1849 to finally crush the insurrection.

WHAT HAPPENED IN NAPLES?

Revolution in Sicily soon spread to the mainland. On 17 January 1848, an uprising of the secret societies in Salerno forced a series of concessions from Ferdinand, including the promise to free political prisoners. But this wasn't enough for most revolutionaries, who also wanted a constitution. A mass demonstration in Naples on 27 January in favour of their demands forced the issue. Ferdinand agreed to grant a constitution. This was due in part to the fact that he was unable to rely on Austrian support as his father had been able to do in 1820 because, as a result of Austrian behaviour in Ferarra, **Pius IX refused to let Austrian troops cross the Papal States**.

ACTIVITY

We have already seen read an extract by Luigi Settembrini (see Source A on page 4). The following source is from his memoirs which were published in 1879.

Source A

As the boat entered the harbour [at Naples] *and prepared to anchor, I saw several ships with tricolour flags, in one was my brother Peppino, who shouted to me across the water; 'Constitution, amnesty, everything has changed, disembark, disembark'. I embraced him and asked him; 'How has all this come about?' 'There was a great demonstration on 27 January and on the 29th was published the royal decree promising a constitution, and giving a full amnesty.' 'Was so much extracted by shouting?' In Naples there has been shouting but in Palermo a terrible revolution which has defeated the troops, and a revolution in Cilento'. 'And Ferdinand, who would rather be a colonel in Russia has yielded.'*

Adapted from Luigi Settembrini, *Memoirs*, 1879

KEY EVENTS

Pius IX refuses to let Austrian troops cross the Papal States In making his decision to deny Austrian troops access to the Papal States, Pius IX even went so far as to ask the Lord to bless Italia. Just the utterance of the word was enough to send nationalists into a frenzy of excitement and adulation. At this point, the papacy really did seem to have put itself at the head of the nationalist cause.

1. In your own words explain Settembrini's account of events.

2. Given what we know of Settembrini, how useful is this extract in explaining the events in Naples in 1848?

The constitution that was issued in February 1848 turned out to be conservative in nature.

- A Parliament was to be created with an upper and lower chamber.
- The King could veto laws and could nominate members to the upper chamber of Parliament.
- A national guard was to be created, albeit under the control of the King.

The granting of a constitution in Naples raised expectation of liberals throughout the Italian peninsula. On 17 February 1848, Grand Duke Leopold granted an equally conservative constitution. In Piedmont, Charles Albert was far less willing to give in to liberal demands. However, he was finally persuaded that it would be better to give in to the limited demands of the more moderate liberals than to risk revolution and the potential of having to face more radical demands. The resulting *Statuto* of March 1848 had great significance in the coming years.

KEY TERMS

Upper house of Parliament Known also as the Senate.

Lower house of Parliament Known also as the Chamber of Deputies.

- It did not grant a full Parliamentary system. The King kept hold of important powers, including the right to sanction laws that had been passed and to appoint the members of the **upper house of Parliament**.
- However, it did create a constitutional monarchy. Parliament was given the right to introduce laws.
- The **lower house of Parliament** was to be elected on a limited suffrage (only 2 per cent of the population). It was given the power to discuss financial issues.
- It guaranteed civil liberties for Piedmontese citizens such as right to religious toleration. It was in granting such liberties that the *Statuto* went further than other constitutions.

With the issuing of the *Statuto*, Pope Pius IX found it difficult to resist calls for a constitution in the Papal States.

The response was limited. He allowed the creation of a
Parliament, but one that had less power than those in the
other states. He also denied the citizens of the Papal States
the basic liberties promised by the Piedmontese *Statuto*. If
contemporaries were looking, here was a clear sign of the
limitations of Pius IX's liberal credentials.

WHAT WAS THE AUSTRIAN REACTION?

The Austrian rulers in Lombardy refused to respond to
agitation for reform. In protest, the citizens of Milan came
up with an interesting way of registering their protest. The
Austrian government held the monopoly over the **sale of
tobacco** in Lombardy. Therefore, the form of protest taken
was a healthy one. The Milanese stopped smoking.
Austrian soldiers and officers seen smoking in the streets
were harassed. In itself, this boycott did not constitute a
full-scale uprising. It was events in Vienna in March 1848
that were to have a considerable impact on what would
happen next. The February revolution in France had
inspired demonstrations in favour of reform in Vienna. As
popular unrest spread, the unthinkable happened. On 13
March 1848, Metternich resigned as Foreign Minister. This
was the trigger for revolution.

The five days of Milan
On 17 March 1848, barricades were thrown up in Milan
and a full-scale battle followed.

- On the one side were the Austrian governor and troops
  with the initial support of the city council.
- On the other was a coalition of anti-Austrian forces.
  These included Mazzinians, liberals, around 100 priests,
  artisans and writers.

In the light of the crisis in Vienna and ferocious opposition
in Milan, the Austrian commander Field **Marshal
Radetzky** took the decision to withdraw his troops to the
safety of the fortresses of the Quadrilatera. The temporary
collapse of Austrian rule left a political vacuum in
Lombardy. The different opinions held in Milan about the
future of Lombardy reflected some of the different strands
of the *Risorgimento* already described.

KEY EVENTS

Sale of tobacco It has been
calculated that the Austrian
government raised the
considerable sum of 5 million
lire a year from taxes on the
sale of tobacco and gambling
in Lombardy. It is likely that a
boycott of tobacco was chosen
as the form of protest because
the secret societies were weaker
in Lombardy.

KEY TERMS

Artisans They formed an
important section of society.
Skilled people and often
literate, they were the
backbone of any uprising.

KEY PEOPLE

**Field Marshal Count
Joseph Radetzky
(1766–1858)** An Austrian
soldier with considerable
expertise in warfare in Italy. He
took part in the military
intervention in 1831 and was
put in command of the
Austrian army in Italy in 1834.
Radetzky introduced strict
discipline into the army he
commanded, but he lacked
resources. In 1848, he was
forced to fall back to the
Quadrilateral. However, in
March 1849 he led his army to
victory at Novara (see page 50).

The street battle at Porta Rosa during the Milan uprising, 22 March 1848.

- The more conservative moderates of the Milan City Council, led by its ***podestà*** Count Gabrio Cassati, feared an independent Lombard republic. Instead they proposed union with Piedmont led by Charles Albert.
- During the uprising, the more radical Milanese formed a Council of War led by Carlo Cattaneo. Their ultimate aim was the creation of a federation of Italian republics.
- A provisional government was formed that was led by Cassati and dominated by the moderates. They knew that the Austrians would be back, so they asked Charles Albert for protection.

Demonstrations in Venice

It was not just in Lombardy that the Austrians were in trouble. In Venice, demonstrations took place demanding the release from prison of patriot **Daniel Manin**. The problem for the Austrians was that many sailors in the Austrian navy docked in Venice were Italian, as were many of the soldiers in the Austrian garrison in the city. Manin was released and, on 22 March 1848, a Venetian Republic was declared. Although Manin preferred Venice to stay independent until the declaration of an Italian Republic, he accepted the vote of the newly elected Venetian assembly to also ask Charles Albert for assistance.

Piedmont declares war on Austria

At first, Charles Albert hesitated to assist. He disliked the revolutionary overtones of what had happened in Milan and Venice. However, one factor above all others convinced him that intervention was the correct course of action. At this moment of Austrian weakness and with Metternich gone, Lombardy was ripe for annexation. Other considerations that helped him to make his decision were as follows.

- He feared intervention of a military force from revolutionary France if he held back.
- He also feared that if he didn't intervene, then revolution in Milan might spread to Piedmont.

On 22 March 1848, Piedmont declared war on Austria. Its army, led in person by Charles Albert, invaded Lombardy. Charles Albert's hope was that he could annex Lombardy without a fight, because the Austrian government was in turmoil. At first it seemed that even if a battle had to be fought, then the Piedmontese stood a good chance of victory. Troops from across Italy converged on Lombardy to join with Charles Albert to purge Italy of the hated Austrians once and for all.

- Columns of soldiers led by General Guglielmo Pepe came from Naples.
- An army led by General Giacomo Durando arrived from the Papal States.

However, Durando had exceeded his orders from Pope Pius IX, who had no wish to fight with Catholic Austria. What happened next very much shaped the course of the *Risorgimento*.

WHAT WAS THE IMPACT OF THE ALLOCUTION, APRIL 1848?

For many conservative Italians, the Pope was the natural leader of Italy. Pius IX had seemingly placed himself at the head of those who wished for an Italian federation under his leadership. However, this was a misreading of Pius IX's intentions. He was not prepared to upset Catholic Austria for the sake of Italian unity. It was not so much Piedmontese anti-clericalism that led to the decline of the papacy's temporal power, but the actions of the papacy itself. A crucial turning point was the issuing of the Allocution in April 1848. On 29 April 1848, in response to General Durando's disobedience, Pius IX issued the famous Allocution; the main points being as follows:

- Pius stated that the war against Austria did not have his blessing.
- He highlighted the fact that Charles Albert was the aggressor in the war.
- The idea of a united Italy was not one supported by the papacy and the Pope did not wish to be considered as the potential leader of any **Italian confederation**.

Italian confederation This was not to be the unified state hoped for by Italian nationalists, but a loose alliance of the kingdoms agreed at Plombières. The Pope was offered leadership in compensation for losing lands to the Kingdom of Central Italy.

The Allocution shocked Italian nationalists. The critical point behind the Allocution of 1848 was that it marked the end of any dream held by moderates and those who ascribed to the ideas of Gioberti and the neo-Guelphs that the Pope might lead the nationalist cause in Italy. It also severely weakened the idea of the Pope as head of an Italian federation, for integral to that role was an element of antagonism towards Austria. In short, it meant that Pius had ruled himself out of the leadership of Italy.

In reality, the Allocution was a statement of neutrality. Pius IX was particularly concerned that his army, led by General Durando, had marched out of the Papal States on 25 April to join the Piedmontese army in its fight against Austria. But if the aim of the Allocution was simply a reaction to this event, then its impact went far deeper. Disclaiming war against Austria severely undermined the papacy's claim to lead the Italian cause. The Allocution was a turning point on the road to a united Italy because it revealed the weaknesses of the papacy's temporal power.

It also weakened Charles Albert's cause as some soldiers in Durando's army would not go against the papal word. Worse was to come for the nationalists with the news on 15 May 1848 that Ferdinand II had re-established autocratic government in Naples. General Pepe was ordered home. He ignored his orders, but many of his troops headed south.

HOW SUCCESSFUL WERE CHARLES ALBERT'S CAMPAIGNS?

Initially, Charles Albert's army was successful in its campaign against Austria. In May 1848, it took Peschiera and won the Battle of Goito. However, the outlook for Charles Albert was distinctly worrying. A French army some 30,000 strong was amassing on the Piedmontese border. Within his own army he had a number of troops left over from Durando's and Pepe's armies, whom he did not trust. Even more alarming was the fact that Radetzky had persuaded the Austrian government to **fight for Lombardy** rather than give it to Charles Albert. On 24 July 1848, the Austrian army overwhelmingly defeated the Piedmontese and their allies at the Battle of Custozza. Radetzky pressed home the advantage, the Piedmontese were expelled from Lombardy by 4 August and the **Armistice of Salasco** was brokered by 11 August.

In November 1848, Prince Felix zu Schwarzenberg was appointed Prime Minister of Austria. This move put paid to any hopes the Piedmontese might have had that the Austrians were prepared to give territorial concessions to prevent future conflict. In Piedmont, Charles Albert was persuaded by Prime Minister Gioberti and General Domenico Chiodo (who took over as prime minister in March 1849) to try one more time to defeat the Austrians. Charles Albert hoped that victory would silence the democrats and republicans in Piedmont whose popularity had increased since the Battle of Custozza. However, the outcome was further humiliation, with Radetzky crushing the Piedmontese army at Novara on 23 March 1849.

In the wake of defeat, Charles Albert abdicated the throne of the Kingdom of Sardinia in favour of his son Victor Emmanuel II. When peace was signed in August 1849, Piedmont was forced to pay reparations of 65 million French francs. The defeat for Piedmont was a humiliating one and was to have important short- and long-term repercussions.

- Before the first campaign against the Austrians, Charles Albert had famously claimed that Italy would *'fare da sè'* ('go it alone'). By this he meant that Italians did not

KEY THEMES

The fight for Lombardy
It was not surprising that Radetzky was keen to fight to hold on to Lombardy. He had spent most of his military career in northern Italy and understood the strategic benefits of holding the Quadrilateral. He also thought his military chances against Charles Albert's army were good. In June 1848, the Austrians ordered Radetzky to seek a negotiated peace. However, he sent Prince Felix Schwarzenberg to Vienna to persuade the government to allow him to fight, which they did.

KEY EVENTS

Armistice of Salasco (1848) Named after the general who brokered the agreement. Charles Albert gave up Lombardy, although the Austrians accepted Anglo-French mediation on the understanding that it might result in territory being handed over to the Piedmontese at a later date. In reality this came to nothing.

need foreign help to get rid of the Austrians. Military defeat in 1848 and 1849 proved Charles Albert wrong. To defeat the Austrians militarily, Italians would need help from abroad.
- The actions of Pius IX had ended the papacy's claim to be the natural leader of Italians. From now on, Italian nationalists treated the papacy as an enemy of Italian unity.
- As the forces of constitutional monarchy and the moderate cause were defeated on the battlefield, so those with a more radical agenda took the initiative.

WHAT WAS THE ROMAN REPUBLIC 1848–9?

With the defeat of Piedmont at Custozza, large numbers of General Durando's troops returned to Rome. Pius IX had issued a constitution in March 1848, but was fearful of a military coup and was now openly unsympathetic to the nationalist cause. In September 1849, Pius appointed Count Pellegrino Rossi as his prime minister, hoping that Rossi would act firmly against liberal reformers and more radical democrats alike. Unfortunately for Pius, Rossi was not popular with the Rome mob and was murdered on 15 November while entering the Roman Parliament. This assassination was the trigger for insurrection against the Pope, who fled Rome on 24 November in fear of his life.

While Pius IX settled into temporary exile in Gaeta in the Kingdom of Naples, power in Rome was exercised by a revolutionary government led by **Giuseppe Galletti**. Although his government was in a difficult position with demands for reform being made from all sides, Galletti's ministry was able to introduce some popular measures in its short period in office.

- The most popular reform was the abolition of the **macinato** in January 1849.
- Also popular was the programme of public works ordered by Galletti's government. This was partly due to the large number of people employed in the building trade in Rome and the desire of the government to keep levels of employment high.

KEY PEOPLE

Giuseppe Galletti A Mazzinian and, in his youth, a revolutionary, Galletti was tried in 1844 for conspiring against Pope Gregory XVI and was sentenced to life imprisonment. Although he was a supporter of Mazzini, Galletti was moderate enough to have been appointed Minister of the Interior by Pius IX before his departure for Gaeta.

KEY TERMS

Macinato A tax that was placed on the grinding of corn. This was highly unpopular in the towns and countryside, where it was seen as taxing a basic necessity as well as driving up the price of bread.

- The government proposed the meeting of a Constituent Assembly, the *Costituente*, to decide the future of Rome and Italy, giving responsibility for the election of the *Costituente* to a **Giunta di Stato**. It was the task of the Giunta to invite the election of deputies from across the whole of Italy, rather than just from Rome.

In January 1849, elections were held in Rome. In February 1849, the *Costituente* met for the first time. Its membership was radical, although mainly middle class. Immediately it announced the end of the Pope's power and the foundation of the Roman Republic. This was not surprising given the popularity of Mazzini's ideas among many deputies in the *Costituente* and it was little surprise that Mazzini was welcomed on his arrival in Rome in March.

The rule of the radicals in Rome was not welcomed by the Pope, nor by his allies across Europe. At a **papal meeting** with his Cardinals in April 1849, he called for foreign support to restore papal power, both spiritual and temporal, in Rome. On news of the defeat of Charles Albert in March, the *Costituente* chose three people to govern Rome. Known as the triumvirate it included Mazzini. In February 1849, the Roman Republic had been declared and Mazzini hastened to Rome. On arrival, he was given power as part of the triumvirate with Carlo Armellini and Aurelio Saffi. Mazzini was the driving force of the government. He ordered the clearing of the Roman slums and the redistribution of some Church land. It was to carry on the reforming work of Galletti's government; for example, the ending of Church control of the press and the abolition of the death penalty. The censorship of the press was abolished, as was the Church's control of education. A constitution was promised. However, it was not issued by the Constituent Assembly until June 1849, by which time it was too late because the republic was on the verge of defeat.

Revolt in Tuscany

It wasn't just in Rome that the democrats raised the prospect of radical revolt. In Tuscany in October 1848, Grand Duke Leopold II was forced to appoint a more 'democratic' government. The new government was led by Professor Giuseppe Montanelli, who wanted a people's war

Giunta di Stato A group of the state. In this case it was made up of three people. They decided that all adult male Romans could vote in the election and that the ballot would be secret.

Papal meeting (April 1849) At this meeting the Pope called on the forces of Spain, France and the Kingdom of Naples to come to his help. He appealed to them by claiming that military intervention was necessary to liberate Rome from 'the enemies of our most holy religion and civil society'.

against Austria. By 1849, the atmosphere had become even more radical and Leopold fled the region. However, the defeat of Piedmont forces at Novara led to the regaining of the upper hand by the 'moderates' and Leopold returned to Tuscany in April 1849.

Threat to the survival of the Roman Republic

Many people in France sympathised with the cause of the Roman Republic. However, Louis Napoleon was able to win over doubters as to the wisdom of the French expedition in 1849 with the explanation that if the French didn't intervene, the Austrians would. He was also playing on the sentiments of significant Catholic opinion in France that wanted to see the Pope restored.

Mazzini's attempt to appease the French

Mazzini hoped that Louis Napoleon might have been persuaded not to attack the Roman Republic and be content with keeping an army in Italy for the purpose of deterring the Austrians from intervening. Measures taken by Mazzini included the return of French prisoners. The policy failed.

How did the Roman Republic end?

The Roman Republic had few friends in Italy or further afield. Neither did it have a significant army with which it could defend itself. The clearest **threat to the survival of the Roman Republic** came from republican France. In France, the president, Louis Napoleon, wanted to win the support of Catholics to send a force to Italy, led by General Charles Oudinot, with orders to crush the Roman Republic. On 24 April 1849, Oudinot landed at Cività Vecchia and marched on Rome. The French were opposed by a makeshift force of volunteers led by perhaps the greatest hero of the *Risorgimento*, Giuseppe Garibaldi. For two months he inspired his troops to block the French army's attempt to take Rome. Meanwhile, **Mazzini's attempt to appease the French** was in the hope that they would not destroy the Roman Republic. By June 1849, the French had amassed an army of 20,000 at the gates of Rome. Garibaldi addressed the *Costituente* promising that the future for Rome's defenders was one of 'hunger, thirst, forced marches, battles and death'. In his last proclamation to the people of Rome on 5 July 1849, Mazzini was unbowed:

An 1849 illustration of 'Garibaldi's men'.

Source A

*'Romans, your city has been overcome by brute force, but your rights are neither lessened nor changed. By all you hold sacred, citizens, keep yourself uncontaminated. Let your municipalities unceasingly declare with calm firmness that they voluntarily adhere to the Republican form of government and the abolition of the **temporal power** of the Pope.'*

Mazzini to the people of Rome, 5 July 1849

ACTIVITY

1. Using Source A and your own knowledge; how do you think historians should judge the period of the Roman Republic?

As the French entered Rome on 3 July, Garibaldi and a force of 4,000 withdrew to San Marino to fight another day. Mazzini made one final appeal to the people of Rome before returning to exile in London. Without doubt the cause of Italian nationalism still fully relied on the attitude of the foreign powers.

What happened in Venice?

Although Charles Albert's army was defeated by the Austrians at Novara in March 1849, the Republic of Venice survived. Thereafter the Republic, led by Daniel Manin, became a symbol of resistance against the Austrians for Italian nationalists. The Venetian rising had little other significance. The rest of Venetia remained under Austrian control and Manin did not have a clear nationalist policy to follow. Most Venetians looked favourably on **Manin's moderation**. He reduced the taxes on important goods such as salt. He also promised universal suffrage. But he managed not to threaten the interests of the middle class or artisans with revolutionary ideas. As a result, they continued to give him their support. Despite being besieged by the Austrian army, and despite hunger and cholera in the city, Venice held out for a year until August 1849, when Manin surrendered.

WHY DID THE REVOLUTIONS OF 1848–9 FAIL?

Lack of support

Although seemingly threatening, the revolutionaries were, in reality, limited in their political and social ambitions. Most of the revolutionaries who came to dominate the revolutions of 1848–9 had the objective of limited constitutional reform. Even Mazzini recognised there was little appetite among the masses for democratic republicanism. There was little significant support for the *Risorgimento* from the peasantry because often those who called for insurrection were seen as more of an opponent than the old regimes. In 1848, the revolutions were mainly urban based in Milan, Rome, Venice, Florence and Turin. The support for these revolutions was drawn from the artisan class. In Sicily, the peasantry invaded the common lands and demanded their restoration. However, they were quickly thrown off the land and the new Sicilian Parliament failed to pass any land reform measures. One reason why the peasantry failed to respond to the call for national unity is that it was based on a Mazzinian idealism that did not go so far as to address the issue of land.

CONCLUSION

The German Karl Marx, wrote that the Roman Republic had been 'an attempt against property, against the bourgeois order'. That 'bourgeois order', both in Italy and elsewhere, stood resolute against the development of Mazzinian principles and the emergence of a democratic Italy.

- But 1848–9 also highlighted the weakness of Mazzinian tactics, the limited support for revolution and the unlikelihood of a 'people's war' to liberate Italy.
- Those who were serious in support of political change in Italy began to look to Piedmont with its liberal constitution and increasingly modern economy. It was also Piedmont that would be most likely to enrol the foreign support necessary to remove Austria.
- Mazzini had created an ideal that threatened those in power. Therefore, over the coming years elements of his message were adopted, distorted, manipulated and mis-

used by the agents of High Politics, most noticeably Cavour. In *Italy: A Modern History* (1959), Denis Mack Smith clearly argues how the pragmatism of Cavour was eventually able to translate 'Mazzini's dogma into practical politics'.

- For Charles Albert of Piedmont and his successor Victor Emmanuel II, the lessons of 1848 were that foreign dominance of Italy could only be ended with outside support. Such support would only be forthcoming if Mazzinianism was kept in check. The process of the unification of Italy from 1848 to 1871 was, in part, as much to do with the defeat of Mazzinianism as it was the creation of an Italian nation state.

- The wars fought by Charles Albert were not wars of national liberation but an attempt to annex territory in northern Italy. Austrian control of parts of northern Italy and influence throughout the peninsula had been challenged but not removed.

- It is clear that the insurrections were mainly regional in nature. Some groups, such as the workers in Venice, hoped for revolutionary change. However, the majority were more conservative in their ambition. The confusion of aims means that it is impossible to generalise that the uprisings were either national or nationalist.

ACTIVITY

There are a number of other reasons why the revolutions of 1848–9 failed. People at the time had their own views as to why the revolutions failed and below is a selection of opinions. Your task is twofold:

1. to read through each source and to summarise the reasons given by sources as to why the revolutions failed

2. to consider the reliability of each source by asking questions based on the following points:

   - the content of the source;
   - the context in which it is written;
   - the situation of the author;
   - the purpose in writing the source;
   - the nature of the evidence.

When you have done that you should attempt to answer the following exam-style 'B' question. Advice on how to answer such questions can be found in the Exam Café on pages 134–139.

Enquiry

Study all the Sources.

Use your own knowledge to assess how far the Sources support the view that the main reason for the failure of the 1848–9 revolutions was the divisions between the revolutionaries.

Source A: Fuller was an American journalist and women's rights activist. She travelled to Europe in 1846 as a correspondent of the *New York Tribune*. Once in Europe she met Mazzini and a revolutionary nationalist called Giovanni Ossoli to whom she became romantically attached. Ossoli fought for the Roman Republic in 1849, Fuller helping tend the republican wounded in a nearby field hospital. Both died in a shipping accident in 1850.

On England no dependence can be placed. She is guided by no great idea. The English traveller, fearing to see the Prince Borghese stripped of one of his palaces for a hospital muses... 'I hope to see them shot these rascally republicans'. How I wish my own country would show some sympathy when an experience so like her own is going on...Order reigns – the same Order that reigned at Warsaw [after the revolution there was crushed]. *Russian-Austrian clemency is yielded to those who remain to share it...The French have not redeemed themselves after their perfidy (treachery)...That intervention, the falsehood of France, the inertia of England, the entrance of Russia into Hungary* [the Russian army crushed the Hungarian Uprising in August 1849] *– all these steps tracked in blood, which causes so much anguish at this moment.*

Adapted from a letter by Margaret Fuller, August 1849

Source B: Nassau William Senior was one of the foremost economists of the nineteenth century. He wrote on a range of political and social issues of the day.

27 November 1850
*I had a long conversation with M. Buonarotti…he spoke with
great bitterness of the republican faction; how Naples' revolt,
the unjust attack on Austria, the insurrections of Genoa,
Leghorn and Florence, has ruined the happiness of this
generation and has thrown back Italy for a century. 'Florence,
Lucca, Sienna, and Pisa all hate one another, even more than
they hate Austria'.*

28 November 1850
*A hopelessly wet day. It was nearly all taken up by a succession
of visitors. First came the Duke Sierra di Falco. He said
'Politics on a grand scale were forced on me* [during the
revolution] *and I don't think that I shall ever take them up
again. Men, at least my countrymen, are not worth the
sacrifices which the attempt to serve them costs. When the
whole united force of all of Italy was not more than was
wanted to drive out the Austrians, we wasted our strength in
civil war, and were never more thoroughly disunited, never
feared and hated one another more deeply, than when we were
proclaiming Italy united.'*

Adapted from Nassau William Senior, *Journals kept in
France and Italy 1848 to 1852*, 1871

Source C: Pisacane was a soldier who fought in Lombardy
in 1848 and 1849. He was a socialist who supported the
idea of linking the cause of national unity to land reform,
something which Mazzini refused to do.

The idea of nationality [in 1848] *was enough to bring about
the uprising but it was not enough to bring victory. The
ordinary people, who wanted to drive out the foreigner* [the
Austrians] *were prepared to accept the leadership of Charles
Albert …* [But] *when other Italian rulers saw that the war
was designed to increase the power of this rival they began to
desert the cause.*

*When the driving force and the overriding principle of
expelling the Austrians failed the ordinary people were left
leaderless. They had no reason to continue to fight, whether*

ruled by a King, President or Triumvirate, the people's slavery does not cease until the social system can be changed.

Adapted from Carlo Pisacane, *Guerra Combattuta in Italia negli anni 1848–9*, 1850–1

Source D: La Farina had been involved in support of the revolution in Sicily in 1848. In this extract he explains to Mazzini why the revolution failed.

No revolutionary government can possess authority or force unless elected by the people. I agree that revolutions are started by minorities but they will collapse unless accepted and organised by the majority. In Sicily the revolution was started by Santoro, later killed by the people as a traitor; Miloro who was then arrested and tried in Sicily for corruption; the Pagano brothers who have become policemen and are cousins of the famous Malvica who was given command of the police when the royalist counter-revolution triumphed in Palermo.

Adapted from a letter from Guiseppe La Farina to Mazzini, 1851

Source E: An extract from the foremost historian of the *Risorgimento* and the unification of Italy.

By the end of 1849 the revolution was over. Venice finally surrendered when an Austrian blockade was made worse by malaria and cholera. Although the Pope returned to Rome, the temporal power was enabled to survive only because [it was] enforced by foreign troops ... The national cause had been advanced, but many weaknesses had been exposed in these two years. Divisions had been opened up between republicans and monarchists, between different regions and neighbouring towns, between federalists and unitarist [those who wanted a unitary state], radicals and conservatives, Catholics and anti-clericals.

Denis Mack Smith, *The Making of Modern Italy 1796–1866*, 1968

CHAPTER 5

What was the significance of political and economic developments in Piedmont 1848–59?

CHAPTER 7

KEY ISSUES

This chapter is important for evaluating the contribution of Piedmont and Cavour for **Key Issue 3** (see page iv).

INTRODUCTION

In 1861 Italy was unified under Piedmontese leadership. There are a number of factors (covered in full later) that explain why this was the case. However, it is wise to start with an examination of why it was Piedmont rather than, for example, the papacy that was to play the central role in forging the new Italian state. The clues in this chapter will be to do with the nature of Piedmontese political system, the strength of its economy and the role played by leading politicians including Cavour and King Victor Emmanual II.

WHY DID PIEDMONT TAKE THE LEADING ROLE?

The Statuto
The reason Piedmont took the leading role in forging political unity rather than any other of the states on the Italian peninsula lies in the nature of Piedmont's political, economic and social development after 1848. The most important feature of Piedmont's political development after 1848 was the retaining of the *Statuto*, first granted by Charles Albert in March 1848. The fact that the *Statuto* survived in Piedmont while the liberal constitutions across the peninsula were repressed was to give Piedmont a crucial edge. From 1849 to 1861 Piedmont acted as a magnet drawing those who wished to live under a liberal constitution. Here it is worth remembering the promises made by the *Statuto*.

- Legislation would be passed by the king in Parliament – that is, with the consent of the king and two chambers (houses) of Parliament (one elected, the other nominated).
- Legislation on taxes would be introduced by the elected chamber of Parliament.

- The press would be free, albeit subject to some restraint.
- Individual liberty was guaranteed.

As a result all of those in Italy who craved political freedom were drawn to Piedmont. In all, perhaps as many as 30,000 exiles moved north to Turin and Genoa in the 1850s. Many were intellectuals who became highly influential in public life – for example, the economist Francesco Ferrara or the writer Giuseppe Massari. Through this movement, Piedmont became the centre of Italian nationalist and liberal thought. Independent newspapers and radical journalism flourished with many writers writing from an Italian, rather than Piedmontese, perspective.

ACTIVITY

Whether King Victor Emmanuel II was so keen on the Statuto is open to question. The following extract gives insight into his thoughts.

Source A

King Victor Emmanuel is in no sense liberal; his tastes, his education and his whole habit of behaviour all go the other way. He tells everyone that 'my father bestowed institutions on the country which are quite unfitted to its need and the temper of its inhabitants' ... Victor Emmanuel does not like the existing constitution, nor does he like parliamentary liberties, nor a free press. He accepts them temporarily as a weapon of war ... Once war is declared [against Austria] *he would suspend the constitution indefinitely.*

Adapted from a letter from the French Ambassador in Turin to the French Foreign Minister, 16 October 1852

1. What, according to the ambassador, is Victor Emmanuel's attitude to the constitution?

2. How reliable is this as an account of Victor Emmanuel's views?

What was the significance of political and economic developments in Piedmont 1848–59?

61

THE SICCARDI LAWS

By the terms of the *Statuto*, the Catholic Church was the established Church in Piedmont. However, many of the Church's power and privileges, which had existed for hundreds of years, were considered by several Piedmontese politicians to be incompatible with various principles of the *Statuto*. In March 1850, a member of the government, Giuseppe Siccardi, brought in a series of bills that were passed by the Piedmontese Parliament. These became known as the Siccardi Laws. The laws controlled the power of the Church. In most states this was done through agreement between Church and state known as a concordat. What made the Siccardi Laws different was that the state passed them without consulting the Church. The range of measures aimed at the Church was broad and the impact far reaching:

- Separate law courts for priests and other ecclesiastical people were abolished, because their existence conflicted with Article 5 of the *Statuto*, which stated: 'All justice emanates from the king.'
- The right of criminals to seek sanctuary and protection in churches was abolished.
- Religious groups, including monasteries, were restricted in their right to buy property.
- The number of feast days on which people were forbidden to work was reduced.

The significance of these laws should not be underestimated. They reflected the determination of Piedmont's rulers to modernise and to assert the dominance of the state over the Church. This was to be a recurring theme of the next few decades.

WHAT WAS CAVOUR'S ROLE IN PIEDMONTESE POLITICS?

Free Trade
In October 1850, Count Camillo Cavour was made Minister of Trade and Agriculture by Prime Minister Massimo D'Azeglio. Soon after, he was given additional

Technological improvement Cavour's technological mind and his interest in all things scientific can be seen in his enthusiasm for the modernisation of the navy.

responsibilities for shipping (a post that included overseeing the operation of the Piedmontese navy), in which his scientific mind resulted in **technological improvement**. In April 1851, he was given the important post of Minister of Finance. He immediately undertook a reform of finances aimed at balancing the books and raising capital for large-scale projects. In late 1851, he borrowed heavily from the London bank of Hambro while increasing taxes. Cavour was a firm believer in free trade and, by the end of 1851, had signed trading treaties with states including Portugal, France, Britain and Belgium. The aim of these treaties was twofold; to ensure both political support and economic growth. The reduction in tariffs resulted in a growth in trade. Between 1850 and 1859, imports and exports increased by 300 per cent.

ACTIVITY

Source A: Cavour justified the introduction of free trade in the following terms.

The system of protection has far more disastrous effects when applied to agriculture than industry. When by means of a protective duty you raise the price of wines and cereals, what follows? With the promise of greater profit, landowners will invest in bringing less fertile land into cultivation. The owners of the land take the profit and, at the same time increasing existing rents at the expense of consumers which means that it taxes consumers for the benefit of the landowners.

Adapted from a speech by Cavour to the Piedmontese Parliament, 8 April 1852

1. What are Cavour's arguments against protectionism?

2. How useful is this extract to the historian investigating the development of Piedmont's economy in the 1850s?

Cavour ordered a new naval vessel from Britain powered by screw propulsion rather than paddle steam. He also introduced metric calibre naval guns.

What was the significance of political and economic developments in Piedmont 1848–59?

Cavour and the Siccardi Laws

As Minister for Trade and Agriculture, Count Camillo Cavour was prepared to speak out in the Chamber of Deputies in favour of the Siccardi Laws. Cavour had been appointed in 1850 to the government led by Massimo d'Azeglio, which could be best described as centre-right in its political leanings. However, the Siccardi Laws marked a divergence of opinion with the more conservative right, led by Cesare Balbo and Thaon de Revel, voting against the first Siccardi Laws. Although the centre-right did not leave D'Azeglio's government over the issue, its disapproval was clear. In December 1851, D'Azeglio attempted to appeal to those on the right by proposing a Press Law that would reduce the freedom of the press. With the Siccardi Laws also under pressure from the Pope, Cavour decided that the time was right for a realignment of Italian politics.

The Connubio

The left minded of Italian politicians had been momentarily discredited with the failure of the 1848 revolutions. At the turn of 1851–2, Cavour made a Parliamentary agreement with the leader of the centre-left, Urbano Rattazzi. The result was the creation of an alliance in the centre of Italian politics known as a *connubio*.

The first consequence of the *connubio* was the clear strengthening of Parliament in relation to the Crown. In May 1852, Rattazzi was elected President of the Chamber of Deputies, despite the king's disapproval. With D'Azeglio's government weakened by the political re-alignment it was not long before his ministry collapsed. In November 1852, Cavour was asked by Victor Emmanuel to become prime minister. As prime minister in the 1850s, Cavour was energetic in his promotion of economic change, but he was also an important influence in the developing nature of the Piedmontese state and the decline in the influence of Mazzini and his followers.

Anti-clericalism

One of the most important aspects of *connubio* was the shared **anti-clericalism** of the centre left and centre right.

The Right Those to the right in Italy in 1850 would be uneasy about far-reaching reform that damaged the Church. They also disliked the policies of free trade. Right-wingers feared revolution and far-reaching reforms. Those to the left, were more sympathetic to reform, and supported a more democratic state and the power of Parliament.

Alliances There were no organised political parties in Italy. Politicians were often elected to Parliament by very small constituencies, generally of around 200 voters. Many politicians were indebted for their political success to important individuals, often landowners. In Parliament, deputies switched allegiances.

KEY PEOPLE

Carlo Pisacane (1818–57) was a writer and a political thinker whose works were to have an important impact on the nature of Italian socialism as it developed. In leading the revolt of 1857, Pisacane attempted to highlight the poor conditions in which the peasantry of the south lived and he hoped to politicise them through his revolutionary example. He killed himself in 1857 when he realised that the insurrection in Naples was bound to fail (he had been injured and over 150 of his followers had been killed). The death of Pisacane robbed the *Risorgimento* of one of its more intelligent and admired leaders.

- On becoming prime minister in 1852, Cavour dropped proposals inherited from the D'Azeglio government in favour of civil marriage. However, his actions were less to do with personal conviction and due more to pressure from the king. Thereafter, Cavour was to pursue a resolutely anti-clerical line. The vast estates of their Church and their generous income of 5 million lire from the state were easy targets.
- In early 1855, Cavour introduced a bill that proposed the abolition of monastic orders not involved in education or charity work. The land belonging to these orders would be taken by the state. The proposal caused a constitutional crisis; it was opposed by Senate, king and papacy. Although Cavour was forced to dilute his proposals (resulting in monks and nuns from closed monasteries receiving generous pensions), he still won, despite being forced at one stage to resign as prime minister.
- In the 1857 election, the candidates of **the right** who had sympathy with the Church increased their vote. Ever the consummate Parliamentary operator, Cavour ended the *connubio* and sacked Rattazzi as Minister of the Interior. He also had to change his attitude to the Church in order to reduce the possibility of **alliances** against his government. The issue of the Church was not raised. However, Cavour's influence was important in identifying mainstream Italian politics with anti-clericalism.

The Radical threat

One of the first issues that Cavour had to deal with was the diplomatic impact of a Mazzinian-inspired insurrection in Austrian-controlled Milan in February 1853. Not wanting to provoke any conflict, Cavour warned Austria of the impending uprising for which he received thanks from Vienna. However, his credentials as a long-term opponent of the Austrians was saved by the next move of the Austrians, which was to seize the property of citizens of Lombardy who had fled to Piedmont. The fury this provoked distracted from the main issue, which was that Mazzini's chosen method of action had again been discredited. This was also the case in 1857, when insurrection in the Kingdom of Naples led by **Carlo Pisacane** was to end in failure. For Cavour, the added shock was that Mazzini led a simultaneous revolt in Genoa

What was the significance of political and economic developments in Piedmont 1848–59?

65

that also ended in failure. Cavour's fury at the futility of such revolutions hid the fact that they were further proof of the unlikelihood of political change in Italy being heavily influenced by Mazzini.

HOW DID THE PIEDMONTESE ECONOMY DEVELOP?

The development of the Piedmontese economy from the mid-1840s should not be underestimated in its significance in relation to Italian unification. As the introduction of the *Statuto* resulted in Piedmont enjoying a distinct political culture, so industrialisation and the building of railways in the 1850s meant that Piedmont was the first Italian region with a partly industrialised economy. As in many other parts of Europe, this industrialisation was based on the building of railways. Its impact was to further the image of Piedmont as a state in the process of modernising (as had the Siccardi Laws).

The Textile Industry

Piedmont's industrialisation did not solely rely on railways. A thriving textile industry based on the manufacture of wool, silk and cotton was firmly established by the mid-1840s. There were severe restrictions to the growth of industry in the north of Italy. In particular, the lack of coal hampered the development of a factory system. Both the wool and silk industries were still predominantly **domestic industries**. They were also labour intensive. The number employed in the silk industries was as high as 60,000 at some points in the 1840s. It was the cotton industry that dominated. Indeed, by 1844 there were approximately 114,000 cotton workers in Piedmont.

The Railways

Further development of the Piedmontese cotton and other industries relied on advances in communication, most obviously the building of railways. The leading proponent of railway building in Piedmont was Cavour. His personal interest in railways would justify him being called an 'enthusiast' and even 'obsessive'. In 1835, Cavour visited Britain to observe the construction of the London to Birmingham railway designed by **Robert Stephenson**. To

Cavour, the material and political benefits of railway construction were clear. In 1845, the Piedmontese government had begun a limited programme of railway construction. In 1846, Cavour wrote an article in the French magazine Revue Nouvelle, which attempted to persuade Charles Albert and his ministers that large-scale railway construction would be of benefit to Piedmont. In his article, he used the following arguments:

- He said the railways were as important as the printing press.
- The railways were inevitable, and their construction in Piedmont would produce economic benefits similar to those experienced in Britain and France.
- The railways would lead to the development of a **national consciousness** and, if Piedmont was that foremost economic power, then it would be identified more closely with a broader national interest.
- Railway construction was underway in Naples, Tuscany and Lombardy. If it was going to lead in Italian railway construction, a commitment was needed sooner rather than later.

It was always Cavour's belief that economic leadership, and railway construction especially, were essential elements of political power. Although Cavour became prime minister in November 1852, he did not lose interest in developing Piedmont's economy. He was also not afraid to use public money and to borrow from abroad to build new railway lines. In 1854, a significant line linking Milan, Turin, Genoa and the French border was opened. This was followed by a commitment to a number of projects, including a proposed thirteen-kilometre railway tunnel through **Mont Cenis**, which gained approval from the Italian Parliament in 1857. The result was that by the end of the 1850s, approximately 850 kilometres of railway track were in operation in Piedmont. This was half the total of track laid in the whole Italian peninsula.

Foreign capital

Cavour encouraged the investment of foreign capital into Piedmont, the majority of it being French. Indeed, the line between Turin and Genoa that was opened in 1854 was

KEY THEMES

National consciousness Cavour was very clear in his belief that railways were of critical importance to the development of Italy as a nation state. He also showed how the absence of railways could be used to stunt development. The best example of this was the failure of the Austrian government to build a rail line in Lombardy up to the Piedmontese border, thereby limiting trade.

KEY IDEAS

Mont Cenis Cavour had great enthusiasm for this scheme. In 1846, he wrote in his article in Revue Nouvelle that such a project would be 'the masterpiece of modern industry'.

What was the significance of political and economic developments in Piedmont 1848–59?

67

funded by French capital, in particular money invested by the bankers Rothschild. Similarly, the Mont Cenis tunnel, started in 1857, was financed by a number of Parisian-based bankers including Laffitte and Rothschild. The importance of such an arrangement should not be underestimated. Influential French finance had an important stake in the financial and economic well-being and expansion of the Piedmontese railways and Piedmont.

Other industry

But it was not just the railways that grew in the 1850s. Government subsidies to a range of enterprises resulted in significant growth. By 1853, the electric telegraph linked Turin to Paris. The building of canals, which began in 1857 with the construction of the Cavour Canal, further boosted the construction industry. However, the result of such government-driven economic modernisation was debt. By 1859, the public debt was 725 million lire. However, such a policy changed the economic status of Piedmont for good. Piedmont was now Italy's foremost industrial region with good trading links to the rest of Europe.

CONCLUSIONS

The 1850s were an important period of political and economic development and change in Piedmont.

- The political system and how it operated was very much conditioned by Cavour's influence and the introduction of the *connubio*.
- One of the effects of the events of 1848–9 was that it encouraged liberals and nationalists to return, or move to Piedmont. This meant that there was an increasing number of people advocating change and led to the formation of the National Society (see Chapter 7).
- Economic and financial reform further enhanced Piedmont's reputation as a modernised state.
- Both political and economic change enhanced Piedmont's role as the potential natural leader of the peninsula and the power most likely to be able to expel the Austrians from Lombardy and Venice.

ACTIVITY

Changes in Piedmont led to changing attitudes towards the state. These two sources are written by people who opposed Piedmontese power in 1848.

Enquiry

Study sources A and B.

> Compare these Sources as evidence for the ideas of Pallavicino and Manin.

Source A: from a letter by Giorgio Pallavicino to General Pepe, 18 November 1851.

I, like you, believe that the life of a people lies in independence more than liberty. But as an Italian first and foremost, I seek Italian forces for an Italian war, and a popular insurrection would not be enough for the purpose.

To defeat cannons and soldiers, you need cannons and soldiers of your own. You need arms, not Mazzinian chatter. Piedmont has got soldiers and cannons; therefore I am a Piedmontese. Piedmont, by ancient custom, tradition, character and duty, is today a monarchy; therefore I am not a republican. And I am content with Charles Albert's Constitution. Independence is the very life of the nation. First independence, then liberty.

G. Pallavicino, *Memorie*, Turin, 1886

Source B: From a letter by Daniel Manin to Lorenzo Valerio.

I am sending you herewith my declaration which has already been published in the Times.

'Convinced that above all Italy must be made, we say to the Monarchy of Savoy: 'Make Italy and we are with you. If not, not.' To the constitutionalists we say 'Be Italian not ***municipalists***. *I think it time to give up existing party divisions; the principal, vital matter is whether we are of the unifying nationalist school of thought or whether we belong to the municipalist school.*

What was the significance of political and economic developments in Piedmont 1848–59?

69

I, a republican, raise the banner of unity. If all those who want Italy gather round and defend it, then Italy will be.

Adapted from a letter by Daniel Manin,
19 September 1855

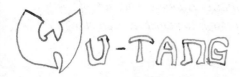

CHAPTER 6

What was the impact of the Crimean War on Italian unification?

INTRODUCTION

The foreign policy that Cavour inherited from D'Azeglio when he became prime minister of Piedmont was well-suited to his political viewpoint.

- Cavour was not an instinctive Italian nationalist. However, he found the attitude of Vienna to northern Italy unsatisfactory. In its treatment of Lombardy, Cavour felt that Austria provoked revolutionaries in and outside the Italian states. Under Cavour, Piedmont foreign policy priorities remained resolutely anti-Austrian.
- Cavour understood that Piedmont could not dominate the north of Italy at the expense of Austria without foreign support. This was to be the cornerstone of his foreign policy.
- D'Azeglio had followed a 'middle-way' foreign policy, which gave encouragement to neither Mazzinians nor **Piedmontese isolationists**, but still hoped to see Austria removed from Lombardy and Venice.
- The Crimean War was a critical turning point in the decline of Austrian power in Italy.

How powerful was Austria?

The slow progress of the cause of nationalism in Italy between 1815 and 1848 was due to the strength and the endurance of Austrian hegemony. The Treaty of Vienna had left the Habsburgs in direct control of Lombardy and Venetia, and Austrian rulers in Tuscany and Modena. The monarchies of the Kingdoms of Sardinia and Naples, and the papacy were restored in the context, and the spirit of Vienna and the nature of their regimes was dictated by Vienna. At the heart of Prince Metternich's foreign policy was a determination to stamp out any revolution and the preservation of the status quo. He also rejected the concept of a liberal constitution and although most restoration

Piedmontese isolationists There were some within Piedmontese political circles in the 1850s such as Solaro della Margherita who believed that Piedmont as a nation would suffer through closer unity with other Italian states.

states were not especially authoritarian, none granted constitutions.

Austrian power and 1848–9

While Austria was strong, the stability of the restoration states was assured. However, the fall of Metternich in March 1848 and the financial crisis that followed it were perceived as signs of terminal decline. But Austrian power in Italy was to remain strong for a time after 1848. Although Austrian forces in Italy were decimated by desertion and were forced, in March 1848, to withdraw to the Quadrilateral, they still were far too strong in battle for anything the Piedmontese and their Italian allies could throw at them. The crushing defeats suffered by the Piedmontese at Custozza in July 1848 and Novara in March 1849, as well as the collapse of the Venetian Republic in August 1849, reflected the continuing strength of Austria. However, it was Pius IX's issuing of the Allocution in April 1848 that revealed the reality of Austrian power in Italy. Even if Pius wished for the expulsion of Austria from Italy, Austria was too strong to be realistically challenged, even in a year of such turmoil as 1848.

Below is a source which gives a clear indication of Austrian attitudes towards the future of Italy.

Source A: An extract from a letter from Field Marshall Radetzky to Austrian Prince Felix Schwartzenberg dated 1849.

In my opinion this wealthy land can only be punished most severely by the removal of those means which have led it to such disobedience, for what is exile to the rich when they can take their money with them and continue to cause trouble.

To humble the disloyal rich, to protect the loyal citizen, but to praise the poorer classes of the peasantry as in Galicia, should be the principle on which from now on the government of Lombardy-Venice should be based.

I am firmly convinced that directly after the conclusion of peace....ringleaders like Casati and Borromeo and others who have suffered punitive justice will petition for clemency and the government will smother them in it. The aim of my letter is, therefore, to beseech Your Excellency beforehand, to set aside any future clemency and let justice run its course completely.

Quoted in A.Sked, *The Survival of the
Habsburg Empire*, 1979

Ultimately, it was Austria's relative decline that made political change possible in Italy. That decline was relative to the increasing power of Prussia and the roots of the change in the balance of power were economic. The development from 1819 of a Prussian-dominated free trade system, the Zollverein, gave the north German states involved an economic advantage over Austria. It was one of a number of factors that led to Prussia challenging Austria's leadership of the loose arrangement of states known as the German Confederation.

In an attempt to challenge Prussian economic dominance in 1849 and 1852 the Habsburgs tried to create a southern Germany/middle Europe equivalent of the Zollverein. The attempt failed. Most of the southern German states such as Silesia were already closely bound into the Prussian-dominated economic system. However, the decline of Austrian political power was not apparent in the early 1850s.

An attempt by Prussia to assert its leadership of at least the north of Germany with the creation of a Prussian League in 1850 led to its humiliation, Austria successfully demanded the disbanding of the League by the Treaty of Olmutz in 1850. Prussia was prepared to back down in the face of Austrian political pressure in 1850 because of the clear superiority of Austrian arms. However, 1850 was the high point of Austrian military hegemony. For the next fourteen years, Prussia consolidated its economic leadership of the Germanic world and by doing so isolated and weakened Austrian power. In 1853, Hanover, Brunswick and Oldenburg joined the Zollverein, thereby completing the economic union of all of non-Austrian dominated Germany.

WHAT WAS THE SIGNIFICANCE OF THE CRIMEAN WAR?

The importance of diplomacy

The importance of diplomacy in forging the shape of the new Italian state should not be understated. The series of events, the change in the balance of European powers and the sympathetic attitude of many of the most significant policy makers at the time would, together, act in favour of those who wished to see the creation of an Italian state.

Under Article 3 of the *Statuto*, foreign policy remained the prerogative of the Crown. As the king's prime minister, this gave Cavour considerable power to make foreign policy as he saw fit and without Parliament's approval. He was determined to exercise this power for the advancement of Piedmontese interests as he saw them. Primarily, these interests were the undermining of the Vienna settlement, thereby weakening Austrian influence in the north of Italy, and the promotion of Piedmontese interests.

Victor Emmanuel II (left), Cavour (centre) and Garibaldi (right). These three men were jointly responsible for the concept of Italian unification.

The Crimea A peninsula in south Ukraine. The main cause of war here was tension between Turkey and Russia over Russian demands for greater influence in parts of the Ottoman Empire. This included demands for control of the Holy Sites in Palestine and the role of protector of Christians within the Ottoman Empire.

KEY ISSUES

The attitudes of Britain and France are important for **Key Issue 4** (see page iv).

KEY THEMES

Cavour's reluctance for war Cavour's reluctance for war reflected the mood of many in Piedmont who opposed the idea of war against Russia when the real enemy was deemed to be Austria. Others such as cabinet member General Vittorio Dabormida opposed going to war without first receiving firm promises of support from the allies.

The cornerstone of Austrian diplomatic strength from 1815 had been the alliance with other conservative monarchies and their shared desire to keep the forces of revolutionary nationalism at bay. Of particular importance for Austria was its alliance with Russia. In 1854 Britain and France declared war against Russia and sent troops to fight in the **Crimea**. Austria remained neutral throughout the Crimean war and, by late 1854, it was clear that Russian antagonism towards Austria was increasing. In August 1854, Austria signed a Four Points agreement with Britain and France aimed at forcing Russia to the negotiating table by the end of the year. For Austria to have acquired such a powerful enemy as Russia was a diplomatic benefit for Piedmont.

Cavour's dilemma

But Austria's close understanding with Britain and France worried Cavour. The military force that Britain and France sent to the Crimea in 1854 was ravaged by cholera. It was therefore very clear to both countries that they would need reinforcements. By mid-1854, the British and French governments placed pressure on Piedmont to join the war. Victor Emmanuel welcomed the pressure placed on Piedmont. By the beginning of 1855, the king had signified that he was prepared to appoint a more pro-war prime minister such as Count Thaon de Revel because of **Cavour's reluctance for war**. In January 1855, Cavour agreed to join the war on the side of the allies (Britain and France). He ordered the despatch of 15,000 troops to the Crimea.

ACTIVITY

Source A: Cavour speaks about why Piedmont should go to war.

Now, gentlemen, I believe that the principal condition for the improvement of Italy's fate is to lift up her reputation once more. And for this it is necessary to prove that her military valour is as great as that of her ancestors. It is our country's task to prove that Italy's sons can fight valiantly on the battlefields where glory is to be won. And I am sure that the laurels our soldiers will win in Eastern Europe will help the future state of Italy more than all that has been done by those who hoped to regenerate her with speeches and writings.

Adapted from a speech by Cavour to the Piedmontese Parliament, 6 February 1855

1. How does Cavour justify Piedmontese involvement in the Crimean War?

2. How reliable is this extract in explaining why Piedmont joined the Crimean War?

War and Peace

The Piedmontese troops arrived in the Crimea in early 1855 but many of her troops were soon struck down with the cholera that had decimated the British army in particular. However, the Piedmontese army did not disgrace itself taking part in the victory over the Russians at Chernaya Rechka on 16 August, which led directly to the fall of Sebastopol. The number of Piedmontese soldiers killed that day, fourteen, does not quite back up the claim of a famous victory. But the battle won the Piedmontese army the respect and gratitude of its allies. In December 1855, Austria threatened to enter the war on the side of the allies and the Russians sued for peace. At the Congress of Paris of February to April 1856, neither Britain nor France was prepared to alienate Austria by addressing any Piedmontese request for a change in the status quo in the north of Italy. However, Cavour did achieve a number of points.

- His attendance at the Congress was a sign of Piedmont's growing diplomatic stature.
- Although Italy was not mentioned until peace had been signed, the 'Italian Question' was the main topic of discussion on 8 April. This was an important step on the road to recognition that Austrian domination of northern Italy was a diplomatic issue.
- The French and British were grateful to Piedmont for its support. This fact would be crucial if and when Piedmont were to militarily challenge Austrian rule.

CONCLUSION

- Piedmontese involvement in the Crimean War was an important diplomatic turning point on the road to national unity.
- The Crimean War and its aftermath marked the end of the Treaty of Vienna and a watershed in Austrian power.
- Austria was now effectively isolated diplomatically. It had lost its great ally, Russia, and was forced to ally with an ultimately unreliable Prussia.
- Neither France nor Britain would, in the medium term, prove to be sympathetic to maintaining Austrian power in northern Italy and its dominant position over the whole peninsula.

ACTIVITY

Cavour was disappointed that the Crimean War ended without Piedmontese soldiers being able to prove their worth on the battlefield. Indeed, he hoped that the military alliance might be continued in war against Austria. He therefore sounded out the opinions of the British representatative at the Treaty of Paris, Lord Clarendon.

Enquiry
Study Sources A and B

> Compare these Sources as evidence for the views regarding British military involvement in the Italian Question.

Source A: Cavour writes about his meetings with Clarendon.

As I went out I told Clarendon 'My Lord, you see we have nothing to hope from mere diplomacy; we shall have to resort to other means, at least over Naples.' He replied 'We must deal with Naples, and soon'.

I have just seen Clarendon. I said: 'Piedmont's position is very difficult. Either we come to an agreement with Austria and the Pope or we prepare to fight Austria ... For the short time that the war lasted, you would have to help us.' Clarendon left off playing with his chin and cried: 'Certainly, certainly, and you could count on enthusiastic, energetic help (from Britain).'

England would with pleasure see an opportunity for a new war, which would be popular because it would be a war for the liberation of Italy.

Adapted from various letters written by Cavour, 9–12 April 1856

Source B: Lord Clarendon recalls his dealings with Cavour in April 1856.

Cavour did not conceal his irritation from me. He constantly told me that he could not present himself before the parliament of Turin unless he had produced some effect by his presence at the Congress. I was in the habit of seeing him daily ... but the substance of our conversations were not of sufficient importance to report to Her Majesty's Government. Consequently there is no record of them nor of my repeated assurances that we would maintain our treaty engagements and to be guided by the principles of international law. At the same time I did not disguise from him that it was our object to free Italy from foreign occupation and reform the Papal and Neapolitan governments, and toward that end the moral support of England would always be forthcoming.

Adapted from Lord Clarendon's speech to the House of Lords, February 1862

What were the roles of Louis Napoleon and Cavour in enhancing Italian unity?

INTRODUCTION

- Cavour and Louis Napoleon are considered to be central figures in the unification of Italy.
- However, their motives and the extent to which they wished to see Italy unified are debatable.
- Other foreign powers were instrumental to unification at certain critical moments.

WHAT WERE THE AIMS OF THE NATIONAL SOCIETY?

Foreign support and diplomacy are often highlighted as the main successes of Cavour. However, his cultivation of the **National Society** was of crucial importance. Formed in the mid-1850s, the membership of the National Society was dominated by Italian exiles living in Piedmont. The aim of the society was to promote the cause of Italian unity. At some time or another, many of its members had supported Mazzini. But by the 1850s, the leaders of the society **Giorgio Pallavicino** and Giuseppe La Farina, plus converts such as Daniel Manin, were prepared to accept that unification might come under the leadership of Piedmontese monarchy rather than as a republic.

In 1856 Manin and Cavour met. At this point, Cavour was still sceptical of unification. But despite the two men not agreeing on the future of Italy, their meeting was another stepping stone on the road to change. In the same year, Cavour met the adventurer Giuseppe Garibaldi to discuss the possibility of war with Austria. Such contacts and the role played by the National Society became very important in later years.

ACTIVITY

This is an extract from the National Society's manifesto which was written by Giuseppe La Farina.

Source A: The 'Political Creed' of the National Society.

Italian independence should be the aim of every man of spirit and intelligence … To obtain political liberty we must expel the Austrians who keep us enslaved. To win freedom of conscience we must expel the Austrians who keep us slaves of the Pope. To recover the prosperity and glory she knew in the Middle Ages, Italy must become not only independent but politically united … We want Rome as our national capital – Rome that peerless town with its glorious history.

We want concord [agreement] between the dynasty of Savoy and Italy, so long as the former wholeheartedly supports the cause of Italian independence.

Giuseppe La Farina, the manifesto of the National Society,
February 1858

1. What are the main principles of the National Society identified in this source?

2. Which potential solutions for Italian unification are implicitly rejected by La Farina in this source?

WHY DID LOUIS NAPOLEON III BECOME INVOLVED?

Dynastic interests

Cavour understood that French support for the removal of Austria would best serve Piedmont's interests. In Louis Napoleon III, he and Piedmont had a potential useful ally. As a 22 year-old, Louis Napoleon had taken part in the uprising in Rome in 1831 and conspiracies in the Papal States and Modena. Such enthusiasm for the romantic notion of Italian liberty and nationalism was to last throughout his political life. Napoleon was grateful to Piedmont for support during the Crimean War and built a close working relationship with Cavour. After the Congress of Paris in 1856, a dialogue was maintained through intermediaries that included Napoleon's nephew Prince Jerome and Cavour's trusted assistant Costantino Niagra. However Napoleon did not act solely with Italian interests in mind.

- As the inheritor of the Bonapartist title, he saw it as his duty to ensure the expansion of France. In particular, he saw the possibility of expanding into **Nice** and Savoy (which were part of the Kingdom of Sardinia) in return for help to expel the Austrians from northern Italy.
- It is possible to interpret Napoleon's help for the cause of Italian unity as being less inspired by romantic ideals and more the hope that, through helping Piedmont assert itself in northern Italy, France would create a client state that would allow it greater influence in that region.
- Napoleon was always wary of Catholic opinion in France. In 1849, he sent French troops to Rome to help crush the Mazzinian-inspired rising and restore the papacy. This move went down well with the Catholics in France. Napoleon never wavered from his commitment to protect the Pope, a commitment that prevented the full unification of Italy until 1871.
- It is also likely that Napoleon envisaged a federation with the Pope at its head rather than the creation of a centralised Italian state. How this would work can be seen in the planning at Plombières (see pages 83–84). There is also little doubt that Napoleon hoped to further the dynastic interests of family members through engineering their appointment to kingdoms in central and southern Italy.

Assassination attempt

On 14 January 1858, four Italians, led by Count Felice Orsini, **attempted to assassinate Napoleon** as he arrived at the opera with his wife, Empress Eugénie. The rationale for such action was that the assassination of Napoleon would lead to the restoration of a republic in France that would be well disposed to the creation of an Italian republic. In the event, Orsini's bomb failed to harm its target; it did, however, manage to kill seven onlookers and

KEY PLACES

Nice The issue of the status of Nice was particularly sensitive. It was feared that if news of the potential transfer of Nice's ownership to France became public it would split opinion in national-minded circles. Most importantly, it would alienate the adventurer, soldier and patriot Giuseppe Garibaldi, who was born in Nice.

KEY EVENTS

Attempted assassination of Napoleon In January 1858, an attempt was made to assassinate Louis Napoleon III. The instigator of the attempt, Orsini, hatched his plans in London, where three large bombs had been made for him. Then he travelled by train to Paris with three co-conspirators (two Mazzinians and a hired assassin). Following a tip-off, the gendarmarie (French police) had been expecting Orsini and his co-conspirators to arrive from England by road. However, the would-be assassins outwitted them by arriving via Brussels.

injure 150 others. From his prison cell, Orsini appealed to Napoleon to actively support the cause of Italian unity.

ACTIVITY

Source A: Part of Felice Orsini's appeal to Napoleon III from his prison cell.

My confession in the trial which followed the attempted assassination of 14 January is enough to send me to my death, and I submit without asking for mercy. Never shall I humble myself before a man who has destroyed the hopes of liberty in my unhappy country. So long as Italy is enslaved, death is a blessing.

However, I make one last attempt to help Italy. Hence these last words are addressed to Your Imperial Majesty..... As a simple individual, I dare to raise my feeble voice from prison, to beg you to give Italy her independence that Frenchmen helped her to lose in 1849. Let me also remind you that neither Europe nor your majesty can expect tranquillity until Italy is free. Deliver my country, and the blessings of 25 million will go with you for ever.

Felice Orsini, 11 February 1858

1. How does Orsini try to persuade Louis Napoleon to help the cause of Italian unity?

2. How useful is this extract to the historian attempting to discover reasons for Louis Napoleon's decision to become involved in Italian affairs (you may wish to answer this question after you have finished reading the chapter)?

It has been assumed that these words in some way created a spark in Napoleon's conscience that triggered him into action and led to the arrangement of a meeting in Plombières on 20 July 1858. This assumption is dubious. Napoleon might have wanted to use Orsini's plea as a romantic cover for what was, in reality, some hard-nosed bargaining.

- Napoleon wished to ensure that there were no further attempts to assassinate him. Therefore, he saw a meeting with Cavour as a way of putting pressure on him to introduce repressive measures against violent nationalists living in Piedmont.
- Napoleon saw this as a chance to deal with a dynastic problem – the difficulties he had had as leader of the Bonaparte family in finding a wife (and role in European affairs) for his cousin, **Prince Jerome Bonaparte**.
- Both Cavour and Napoleon wished for **war against Austria**. A potential problem was that their motives for war differed. Cavour wanted war to remove Austrian influence from northern Italy. Napoleon wanted war to gain territory but also as part of a broader diplomatic strategy regarding Austria.

Plombières

It was agreed at the secret meeting in Plombières that France would join Piedmont in war against Austria, if war could be provoked in a way acceptable to opinion in the two countries. The aim, of course, was to use military force to drive Austria out of Italy. Other terms of the agreement were as follows.

- A Kingdom of Upper Italy (ruled by the House of Savoy) would be created to cover the provinces of Piedmont, Lombardy and Venetia, and the duchies of Parma, Modena and the Papal Legations.
- A Kingdom of Central Italy would be controlled by Tuscany, and would also include Umbria and the Papal Marches.
- Rome and the surrounding area would remain in the control of the papacy and the Pope would lead an Italian confederation.
- For the present time, the Kingdom of Naples would remain as it was. This was mainly because Napoleon feared that to unseat the Bourbons might upset the tsar, who saw himself as an ally of this similarly autocratic dynasty.
- In return for the support of 200,000 French troops, Napoleon demanded Savoy and Nice. Cavour was quite happy to accede to the request for Savoy, the majority of its population being French speaking. However, this was

not the case in Nice and it took until January 1859 for Piedmont to agree.

- More important for Napoleon, the agreement was to be sealed with the marriage of the fifteen year-old Marie Clotilde (daughter of the Italian king, Victor Emmanuel II) to the middle-aged Prince Jerome Bonaparte.

HOW SUCCESSFUL WAS WAR WITH AUSTRIA, 1859?

War is provoked

The problem for Cavour was how to provoke war with Austria in such a way that his and France's ambitions were not made too obvious. In his opening of Parliament on 12 December 1859, **Victor Emmanuel** delivered a deliberately provocative **speech**, but to little effect. This was the least of Piedmont's worries. At Plombières, Cavour had promised to match Napoleon's promise of an army of 200,000 with a force of 100,000. However, by the turn of 1858–9 this was proving hard to find. The National Society recruited some 20,000 volunteers, but many of these men were untrained and no match for the Austrian army. The army reserves Cavour hoped to mobilise did not exist. In the end, the Piedmontese army numbered around 60,000.

- There was no popular enthusiasm for war. In 1848–9, **war against Austria** was seen by many as a popular crusade. This time, though, things were very different, the war being engineered by Cavour.
- A war in northern Italy was unpopular with other European powers. The Prussians made it clear that their sympathies would be with Austria, although the Russians had assured France of their neutrality and goodwill. In Britain, the prime minister, Lord Derby, and his foreign secretary, Lord Malmesbury, were sympathetic to the cause of Italian unity, but did not wish to see a war deliberately provoked. To many, Austrian domination in northern Italy would be replaced by French domination, which was equally undesirable. They pressed for a Congress of European powers to resolve the issue. To Cavour's horror, it seemed that Napoleon was

KEY IDEAS

Victor Emmanuel's speech In his speech, he threatened: 'For while we respect treaties we are not insensitive to the cry of anguish that reaches us from so many parts of Italy.'

KEY THEMES

War against Austria in The Risorgimento (1959) Agatha Ramm argued that '*Napoleon was almost equally as much a liability as an asset*' to the cause of Italian unity. His desire to go to war against Austria in 1859 was not to relieve the '*cries of pain*' but as Ramm argued '*to draw diplomatic profit from the war*'.

increasingly convinced of the desirability of a peaceful solution to the Italian question.

However, as the diplomatic manoeuvrings continued, so tension increased. In March 1859, the Piedmontese army was mobilised. The Austrians followed suit in April. The problem for the Austrians was that, having mobilised, they now needed to either use their army or demobilise, which would be costly. Therefore, on 23 April the Austrians demanded Piedmontese demobilisation within three days. When it was not forthcoming they declared war and, on 29 April, troops under General Franz Gyulai invaded Piedmont. However, the Austrian army was delayed by poor weather, which gave the French plenty of time to move their army by rail into Piedmont.

Change in the Grand Duchies

Events moved fast in the Grand Duchies, manipulated by the National Society that forced the pace of change.

- In April 1859, in Florence there was a popular demonstration against the Grand Duke Leopold that resulted in his flight and the creation of a provisional government led by **Baron Bettino Ricasoli** that favoured union with Piedmont.
- In May 1859, the National Society engineered peaceful revolutions in Modena and Parma, and the rulers fled leaving provisional governments in control.
- In June 1859, the Duke of Modena and the Duchess-Regent of Parma fled their provinces. They were replaced by a government led by **Luigi Farini**, which was, again, close to Piedmont. Indeed, government under Farini was akin to being ruled as a Piedmontese colony, because all major governmental decisions were approved in Turin.

There was further political unrest when, in June, insurrections took place in the **Papal Legations**. In Bologna (the capital of the Papal Legations), Piedmontese commissioners moved in to restore government. Most of these commissioners were members of the National Society. Only in Tuscany was there any demonstration of popular support for a change in government.

KEY PEOPLE

Baron Bettino Ricasoli (1809–80) A strong supporter of the cause for Italian unity. In 1859, he became the leader of the Tuscan government after Grand Duke Leopold II. ed. He arranged the annexation of Tuscany to the Kingdom of Sardinia. After unification, Ricasoli was twice Prime Minister of Italy, in 1861–2 and 1866–7.

Luigi Farini (1812–66) Once the private physician to Prince Jerome Bonaparte, Farini entered politics in the 1840s.

KEY TERMS

Papal Legations These were made up of the provinces of Ravenna, Ferrara and Bologna.

Despite these events, the political future of these provinces relied, in the short term, on events on the battlefield.

The battles

Minor victories by the Piedmontese army at Palestro and by Garibaldi's *Cacciatori delle Alpi* at Como in May 1859 helped to pave the way for the two large-scale battles of the war at **Magenta** (4 June) and **Solferino** (24 June). The Austrians were defeated at both battles, but the margin of victory for the French and Piedmontese was narrow. The Austrians still held the Quadrilateral and showed no sign of withdrawing from northern Italy. Indeed, there was little prospect of the French and Piedmontese defeating the 150,000 strong Austrian army, which was well entrenched without considerable bloodshed.

WHY DID NAPOLEON SUE FOR PEACE?

Napoleon's ambition to have freed Italy 'from the Alps to the Adriatic' seemed unlikely to be fulfilled in the short term. So, without Cavour knowing, he sued for peace with Austria. An armistice was proposed by Napoleon on 8 July 1859. This was followed by a meeting at Villafranca on 11 July between Napoleon and the Emperor Franz Joseph. Apart from his distaste for the bloodshed, Napoleon had other motives for making peace behind Piedmontese backs.

KEY TERMS

Cacciatori delle Alpi
Translated as 'Alpine Hunters', this group could be described as a private army led by Garibaldi. Around 3,000 strong, they were volunteers and highly effective in their work.

KEY EVENTS

Battles of Magenta and Solferino These battles mark a turning point in warfare. With the advent of new and more accurate weaponry, the deployment of large armies on the battlefield was a recipe for carnage. Despite the carnage at both battles, there was only one doctor per 500 casualties on the allied side.

Painting of Napoleon III at Solferino, 1859, by Beauce. The picture shows the carnage on the battlefield.

**Lord Palmerston
(1784–1865)** Palmerston
originally became a Tory
Member of Parliament in 1807.
He joined the Liberals in 1830,
and was prime minister from
1855 to 1858, then again from
1859 to 1865. Palmerston
made it known that he was
anti-Austria south of the Alps
(that is, in Italy), but pro-
Austria north of the Alps.

**Lord John Russell
(1792–1878)** Russell first
became a Member of
Parliament in 1813. He was
prime minister from 1846 to
1852. He became Lord
Palmerston's foreign secretary in
1859. Russell was a strong
supporter of Italian unification,
as were most Liberals at the
time. He was also a believer in
free trade and argued that a
free, united Italy would be a
strong trading partner for
Britain. His belief that the
Italian Question should be
solved by applying the idea of
self-determination was echoed
by the President of the United
States of America, Woodrow
Wilson, at the end of the First
World War some 60 years later.

Prussia Prussia was willing to
support Austria as long as it
was allowed greater influence
among the organisation of
German states known as the
German Confederation.

**Napoleon I and the
coalition** By the end of the
Napoleonic Wars in 1815,
Napoleon I faced a coalition
that included Britain, Prussia,
Austria and Russia.

- Napoleon disapproved of the turn of events in central Italy. He felt that the papacy was under threat with a National Society government-friendly to Piedmont in Bologna. He also felt that Piedmontese control of central Italy went beyond the points agreed at Plombières. Napoleon was embarrassed by the demands of French Catholics for him to act to rectify a situation that was clearly getting out of hand.
- On 24 June 1859, the Prussian army mobilised an army on the banks of the Rhine. Fearing that the British government would fail to support him, Napoleon sued for peace with the Austrians at Villafranca. Although Prussia was not the threat it would be ten years later, mobilisation of its army on the Rhine was enough to push Louis Napoleon into the arms of the Austrians. To the satisfaction of the Austrian emperor, Franz Joseph, the Prussians were made to 'look foolish', but he missed the point. The threat of Prussian intervention was enough to bring Napoleon to the negotiating table.

Foreign disapproval

In *The Struggle for Mastery in Europe 1848–1918* (1954), A.J.P. Taylor wrote: 'Italy owed most to French armies and British moral approval.' The coming to power in Britain in June 1859 of the second ministry led by **Lord Palmerston,** with **Lord John Russell** as Foreign Secretary, had an important impact on the process of unification. Not all British politicians were keen to see the creation of a united Italy, but Palmerston and Lord John Russell, definitely were. Neither politician wished to see the maintenance of Austrian power in northern Italy and both were adamantly opposed to any extension of French interest in the region. However, they were restrained by domestic considerations (including the views of Queen Victoria) and maintained a policy of strict neutrality. Louis Napoleon faced a potentially worrying problem as events unfolded in the summer of 1859. The government in **Prussia** made it known that it might lend some support to Austria by mobilising its armies along the River Rhine, thereby threatening France. The outline of a **coalition** as faced occasionally by his uncle **Napoleon I** was becoming ominously clear to Napoleon III and was to be avoided at all costs.

VILLAFRANCA

At Villafranca, Piedmont's ambitions were forced to play second fiddle to the diplomacy of Napoleon. Some aspects of Plombières survived, but many did not.

- Austria agreed that Lombardy should be given to France, which might then choose to give it to Piedmont in due course. However, Venetia was to remain in Austrian hands.
- Piedmont was not to be given control of Modena or Parma and the rulers who had been forced to flee from the central Italian states were to be restored. Piedmont was also forbidden to annex Mantua and Peschiera in Lombardy.
- An Italian confederation was to be set as up, as agreed at Plombières, with the Pope at its head.

KEY ISSSUES

The moral approval of Britain is important for **Key Issue 4** (see page iv).

The unification of Italy, 1859–71.

The effect on Cavour was predictable. He resigned his post as prime minister and was not present at the signing of the Treaty of Zurich in November 1859, which formally ended the war. As part of the treaty, Napoleon suggested that the issue of central Europe be decided by a Congress of the European powers. This was a compromise that did not please the Piedmontese government, now led by Alfonso Lamarmora.

THE POPE AND THE CONGRESS

Despite agreeing at Villafranca that the rulers of the central Italian states should be restored, Napoleon accepted later in the year that the decline in the Pope's temporal power was inevitable. In December 1859, a pamphlet written on behalf of Napoleon and entitled *The Pope and the Congress* was published in Paris. In it, Napoleon suggested that he would be prepared to accept that the Pope should lose control over the Legations. This was the crucial turning point on the road to unification. By accepting a decline in papal power, Napoleon upset Catholics in France and the Austrians. But he very much pleased the British. The main consequence of the pamphlet was that the idea of the Congress was dead. It was the British foreign secretary Lord John Russell who seized the moment. He proposed that the future of the Italian peninsula should be decided through the application of the principle of **self-determination**. This was another crucial moment. Cavour returned as prime minister on 21 January 1860 and negotiated a deal, the Treaty of Turin, with Napoleon.

- Piedmont would hand over **Savoy and Nice** to France.
- France would accept Piedmontese annexation of the central Italian duchies, as long as the annexation was accompanied by plebiscites (popular votes).

TREATY OF TURIN

At Plombières, Cavour had been reluctant to discuss the French annexation of Nice because he was aware that the reaction of those nationally minded to the loss of an Italian dialect-speaking province would be considerable, especially to Garibaldi who was born in Nice. However, at the Treaty of Turin in March 1860, Cavour was content to sign over Savoy and Nice to France in return for Lombardy and French recognition of the plebiscites outlined on page 95. This was despite the fact that he was not obliged to do so by the terms of the Plombières agreement, as Louis Napoleon had failed to keep his side of the bargain and push the Austrians out of Venice. However, his diplomatic instincts were sufficient to tell him that the key to Piedmontese strength was the continual support, however erratic, of Louis Napoleon.

Cavour was a pragmatist. He was also politically astute. His defining and most significant attribute was his ability to respond to events and to understand the opportunities that these events presented to Piedmont. The clearest case in point was the issue of the annexation of the central Italian duchies by Piedmont in March 1860. Such an annexation was not foreseen by Cavour or Louis Napoleon at Plombières. Neither was the annexation particularly acceptable to the French, given the fact it changed the balance of power foreseen by Plombières and, thereby, reduced the possibility of French influence. Hence Cavour's willingness to sign the Treaty of Turin and the surrendering of Nice to France.

CONCLUSION

Louis Napoleon and Cavour played crucially important roles in enhancing the cause of Italian unity. They had different reasons for promoting change: Louis Napoleon wished to secure dynastic interests and French power, Cavour wished to enhance the position of Piedmont. Neither could foresee the consequences of their actions and, as is suggested in the following two sources; their viewpoints on the future of Italy were in fact quite different in the mid 1850s.

ACTIVITY

Read Source A and then answer the following questions:

- To what extent did Louis Napoleon implement the ideas proposed in this memorandum?
- How useful is such a piece of evidence to an historian trying to discover Louis Napoleon's true motivation for interfering in Italian affairs?

Enquiry
Study Sources A and B.

Compare these Sources as evidence for the thoughts about the future shape of Italy.

Source A: An extract from a memorandum written by Louis Napoleon in March 1856 to himself and his Foreign Minister Count Walewski.

The aim of all statesmen must be to avoid, as much as possible, all the ferments of dispute that still exist in Europe. Now one only has to open one's eyes to see that the country which is the greatest threat to European peace is Italy. To alter its structure either a revolution or a war is needed – two fatal extremities; and in any case who would be powerful enough to impose his will on so many divided countries.

Nonetheless I believe that one might try something that might satisfy nearly everyone. An Italian Confederation might be set up, under the nominal leadership of the Pope, on the model of the German Confederation, i.e. a diet, appointed by the various States, could meet at Rome and discuss matters of common interest without any change to territorial boundaries or the rights of various rulers. The Diet would not only deal with the major issues of general interest to Italy…but it would have some administrative powers…Each State would have one vote or representative for every one million inhabitants.

Source B: A letter from Giorgio Pallavicino to Daniel Manin 1856.

Piedmontism is for us an extremely dangerous opponent, an implacable enemy. Everyone in Piedmont – from Count Solaro della Margarita to Angelo Broferio – is tarred with this same brush. Instead of a single Italian nation with its centre in Rome, they would prefer a Kingdom of northern Italy with two capitals, Turin and Milan. Camillo Cavour is one of the most Piedmontese of all and we shall harness him to our chariot only when we have a knife at his throat.

CHAPTER 8

How did Cavour and Garibaldi shape Italian unification, 1859–60?

INTRODUCTION

The events of 1860 were to transform the creation of an expanded north Italian state into the unification of the Italian peninsular, something which was inconceivable only a few years before. The actions of Garibaldi and the response of Cavour in this period were essential to the shaping of Italian unification.

In this chapter you will see how the actions of Garibaldi led to the creation of an Italy which included virtually all of the Italian peninsular, rather than a northern Italian state as envisaged by Cavour. However, you will also see how Italy was unified under the Piedmontese monarchy as hoped for by Cavour and Victor Emmanuel, rather than as a Republic. The new Italian state of 1860 was a conservative settlement although Garibaldi's daring exploits were to provide the *Risorgimento* with its greatest hero. The tension and competition between Cavour and Garibaldi (with help from Victor Emmanuel) was to shape the new Italian state.

HOW WERE THE CENTRAL STATES ANNEXED?

In order to legitimise the annexation of central Italy, Cavour came up with the idea that it should take place through popular consent. Such an idea was, of course, a direct contradiction of his real beliefs. The idea of self-determination, that the peoples of Italy would determine their own future, smacked of Mazzinianism. However, Cavour was wise enough to realise that he could borrow the language of popular change and some of its trappings (for example, plebiscites) for his own ends. Cavour understood that the idea of holding plebiscites would be acceptable to the British government led by Lord Palmerston and Bonapartist France, and he was right. He also understood that the votes could be fixed through intimidation, corruption and bullying. The fact that there was an organisation, the National Society, willing to do Cavour's dirty work made it much easier for him to distance himself from some pretty strange results.

Despite Villafranca, Grand Duke Leopold did not return to power in Tuscany. Instead, power was held by Baron Ricasoli, who had engineered the election of a subservient local assembly, which, in August 1859, had voted to ask for annexation by Piedmont. Meanwhile, Ricasoli exercised power as a dictator. In Emilia, Farini had remained equally powerful. The plebiscites were an opportunity for them to engineer annexation with the help of the National Society, which campaigned enthusiastically. All males over 21 were given an opportunity to vote. Their choice was:

- annexation to the constitutional monarchy of Victor Emmanuel II, or
- a separate kingdom (the nature of the 'separate kingdom' remaining deliberately vague).

ACTIVITY

Source A: An extract from the diary of Marco Tabarrini who was a close collaborator of Baron Ricasoli.

10 March 1860: Great enthusiasm for tomorrow's elections, especially in the provinces. Though the people may not have realised the importance of the vote, they are proud that they have been called to exercise a new right. I heard a shoemaker say, 'Tomorrow I'm worth as much as Prince Corsini [a prince from one of the most famous noble Tuscan families]'.

Alberi has published a protest invalidating the suffrage, saying it is not free. Actually he is wrong, because though admittedly there's a farcical element in it, universal suffrage will be as free in Tuscany as elsewhere.

1. What does Tabarrini suggest is the mood surrounding the election?

2. How reliable is this extract for the historian researching the plebiscites of March 1860?

Plebiscites The voting figures from the plebiscites are so one-sided that the historian Martin Clark wrote in *The Italian Risorgimento* (1998): 'Hitler and Stalin in their heyday never received results like this.'

When the elections took place in March 1860, it was clear that there was widespread vote rigging. It was little surprise that the **plebiscites** resulted in a crushing victory for those in favour of annexation. The votes were as follows.

	For annexation	Against annexation
Tuscany	386,445	14,925
Emilia	427,512	756
Savoy (to France)	130,583	235
Nice	24,448	160

In reality the plebiscites were a charade, and Cavour's government had hidden behind the cloak of popular suffrage. The annexations were the result of the diplomacy and the skills of the National Society and the Piedmontese commissioners in the central Italian states.

WHO WERE GARIBALDI'S 'THOUSAND'?

What happened next was to turn the annexation of central Italy by Piedmont into the unification of the peninsula. The reaction of Garibaldi to the surrender of his birthplace,

An 1863 painting by Borrani entitled 'The Sewing of Red Shirts'. The picture shows a group of women preparing shirts to be worn by the volunteers of Garibaldi's army, otherwise known as The Thousand.

Nice, to the French was to organise a force to prevent its annexation. The group that became known as 'The Thousand' met near the port of Genoa. As the group increased its numbers, news broke in April 1860 of an insurrection on the island of Sicily. Although about only one-tenth of Garibaldi's force were Sicilian, he was persuaded by two of his most trusted followers, **Francesco Crispi** and Rosalino Pilo, to sail south. Garibaldi concurred. On 12 April, Pilo sailed on ahead to rally the Sicilian revolutionaries and inform them that help was close at hand.

Once at sea, Garibaldi declared that he was going to liberate Italy in the name of 'Italy and Victor Emmanuel'. The Mazzinians among The Thousand were reluctant to give their allegiance to a monarchy, but this reluctance was tempered by Mazzini's acceptance in March 1860 of Victor Emmanuel as leader of a united Italy if that was the popular choice. As Garibaldi headed south, so Cavour was faced with a difficult dilemma.

ACTIVITY

Source A: Adapted from a letter from Cavour to his representative in Paris, Costantino Nigra, May 1860.

I regret Garibaldi's expedition and I am doing everything possible to prevent it causing new complications. I did not prevent Garibaldi carrying out his project because that would have needed force. Moreover the government is in no state to face up to the enormous unpopularity it would have incurred by arresting Garibaldi. Another consideration was that elections are imminent, and I need the support of all shades of the moderate liberal party if we are to get the French Treaty [Treaty of Turin] passed. I did everything in my power to persuade Garibaldi not to go on his mad escapade. I sent La Farina to talk to him, who came back with an assurance that the whole idea was off.

1. What are Cavour's concerns about the actions of Garibaldi and the 'Thousand'?

2. Have we any reason to doubt the validity of this extract?

The Thousand There were actually more than 1,000 volunteers who rallied behind Garibaldi. More than half the forces were from Lombardy. Many were students with a few professionals and workers involved. Several volunteers wore red shirts to symbolise their willingness to spill blood in the name of Italy – hence their nickname 'Garibaldi's Red Shirts'.

Francesco Crispi (1819–1901) Crispi had taken part in the uprising in Sicily in 1848 and thereafter went into exile. He returned in 1860 to join Garibaldi's expedition to Sicily. He became a politician in the new state and was elected to be a deputy in the Italian parliament in 1861. Crispi was twice Prime Minister of Italy, from 1887–91 and 1893–6, and became one of the most significant prime ministers of the new Italian state.

Garibaldi lands in Sicily
For a short while Garibaldi
acted as ruler of Sicily, which
was no easy task. At first he
sought to please the peasants
by abolishing the grist tax, a
tax on milling corn. However,
widespread unrest led him to
use force to restore law and
order to the relief of the
nobility.

**Giuseppe La Farina:
Cavour's agent** This was a
strange choice for Cavour to
make. La Farina was highly
influential as leader of the
National Society. However, he
was in favour of the French
being given Nice, which didn't
exactly endear him to
Garibaldi. Indeed, La Farina's
behaviour convinced
Garibaldi that Cavour was out
to stop him invading the
Italian mainland.

On 11 May 1860, **Garibaldi landed in Sicily** but met little opposition. The ranks of The Thousand were swelled with new Sicilian recruits as they marched on Palermo. Garibaldi's Thousand may well have been poorly armed with dated muskets. However, they were experienced, well trained and Garibaldi was a first-rate military commander. The first encounter with the Neapolitan army at Calatafimi on 15 May resulted in a sensational victory for Garibaldi's troops. Palermo was taken later in the month. The island of Sicily was conquered by the end of July.

How did Cavour try to contain Garibaldi?

It is clear that throughout the episode, Cavour struggled to regain control of the situation. If he was seen to help Garibaldi he would run the risk of alienating France and moderate opinion in Piedmont, which feared the consequences of Garibaldi's revolutionary activity. If he refused to support such a popular adventure he would be seen to be restraining action undertaken in the Italian interest. However, Cavour did work out another policy, that of interference through agents. He sent his agent, **Giuseppe La Farina**, to Sicily to claim its annexation to Piedmont. However, Garibaldi was not quite ready to hand over his hard-fought gains just yet and La Farina was sent away empty-handed. Another more acceptable envoy, Agostino Depretis, was despatched instead. None the less, he failed to stop Garibaldi embarking for the mainland on 19 August.

For Cavour the danger was that the situation was developing out of his control. At this stage, he still did not envisage a unified Italy including the south. Even more worrying for Cavour was that Garibaldi might initially aim to invade Naples, although he knew that his ultimate target was Rome. But any threatening of Rome would result in opposition from the French, and Cavour realised that any resulting conflict would end in a French victory.

The British, however, were sympathetic to Garibaldi's expedition, and the crossing of the Straits of Messina was undertaken under the watchful and sympathetic eye of the Royal Navy. Those wishing to stop Garibaldi now attempted to act, but their efforts were too little too late.

Portrait of Count Camillo de Cavour by M. Gordigiani.

Giuseppe Garibaldi at Caprera in 1865.

Cavour ordered Admiral Persano of the Piedmontese navy to sail to Naples and organise a pro-Piedmont insurrection before Garibaldi arrived in the city. He failed. In the face of Garibaldi's success, Cavour had to reassess his attitude to the whole episode.

Prompted by Louis Napoleon, Cavour worked behind the scenes for an alliance with the Bourbons against Garibaldi. In June 1860, he sent messages to King Francesco of Naples suggesting an alliance. At the same time, though, his agents were working hard in Naples attempting to provoke an uprising against the Bourbons that would justify Piedmontese intervention. Although he was prepared to entertain the possibility of a united peninsula, he was not prepared to accept it as a democratic Italy. Garibaldi launched his invasion of the Italian mainland in August 1860 in the name of 'Victor Emmanuel and Italy'. However, it was not the Italy envisaged by a far more conservative Cavour.

It was Cavour's ability to gamble when necessary that secured the Italy of his liking. As Garibaldi's **invasion of the mainland** proved to be a success, so the urgency of the situation for Cavour became even greater. It was important

KEY EVENTS

Invasion of Naples After Ferdinand fled Naples, the city was governed by democrats sympathetic to Garibaldi's cause. Therefore, instead of having to besiege or attack the city he took the train to Naples, receiving a hero's welcome at the station.

Cavour seen to supplort Garibaldi On 9 August 1860, Cavour wrote: 'Garibaldi has rendered Italy the greatest services that a man could give her: he has given Italians confidence in themselves. He has proved to Europe that Italians know how to fight and die on the battlefield to reconquer a fatherland.'

Winners and losers In 1948, the historian Gaetano Salvemini wrote in *Mazzini* (1948) that the unification of Italy was not the result of a harmony of ideas born of the *Risorgimento* but of a struggle: *'In reality there was in the struggle a winner and a loser; the winner was Cavour, the loser Mazzini.'*

Sir Robert Peel (1788–1850) and Machiavelli (1469–1527) Robert Peel was an English statesman. He was prime minister twice between 1834 and 1846. Machiavelli was a political philosopher. The quote from Mack Smith refers to Cavour being compared by the deputy to a much admired and competent British prime minister as well as the master of the art of political intrigue.

for **Cavour** that he **was seen to support Garibaldi**. The king and many in the Piedmontese Parliament hailed Garibaldi's actions in liberating the south from the rule of the despotic Bourbons.

Garibaldi and his troops took Naples in early September. Cavour feared that Garibaldi would now march on Rome. The threat of such an invasion was real. Not only did Garibaldi possess a force some 20,000 strong (and possibly greater), but also a force some 9,000 strong led by Agostino Bertani (a supporter of Mazzini) had amassed on the border of the Papal States. Cavour's clear option was to invade the Papal States in order to forestall any further action on Garibaldi's behalf. Even if this meant upsetting the Pope and possibly the French, it was a risk Cavour felt he should take.

As Garibaldi planned his invasion of the Papal States, Cavour acted. The National Society engineered an uprising in the Papal States on 8 September. Cavour demanded that the papal army be disbanded rather than suppress the uprising.

The problem for Cavour was that the uprising was a damp squib, and a number of powerful voices inside Piedmont (for example, D'Azeglio) and abroad (for example, the governments of Spain and Portugal) complained that Cavour was acting in breach of international law. However, he ignored such protests and the Piedmontese army invaded the Papal States from the north on 11 September 1860. Napoleon was aware of the invasion and did not object as long as the Piedmontese army avoided Rome. On 18 September, the papal army was destroyed at the Battle of Castelfidaro. However, the Neapolitan army was still intact. Garibaldi's task was to defeat this army, thereby opening the way to a convergence of forces fighting in the name of Victor Emmanuel II. Victory was achieved on 26 October 1860 at the Battle of Volturno.

In *Italy: A Modern History* (1959), Denis Mack Smith points out how a deputy of the Italian Parliament referred to Cavour as 'a cross between **Robert Peel and Machiavelli'**. He stressed, quite correctly, that Cavour's actions in 1860 were not of a man with a desire to see Italy unified. Indeed, he acted because, as Mack Smith pointed out, *'he disliked revolutionary republicanism more than he loved national unity'*. As a result, he responded to Garibaldi's invasion of the mainland with a strategy aimed at *'outdoing* [the revolutionaries] *at their own game'*.

How was the issue settled?

Meanwhile, plebiscites were arranged in the south with the simple question: 'One Italy, Victor Emmanuel: yes or no?' The result was not surprising, although enthusiasm for the Piedmontese king was limited. Most Sicilians and Neapolitans were voting for the end of the feudal monarchy of the Bourbon family.

The voting figures for the plebiscites held on 21 October were as follows:

	Yes	No
Sicily	432,053	667
Naples	1,302,064	10,312

These were followed by plebiscites arranged in the more northerly provinces of the Marches and Umbria that were held in November 1860. The voting figures for these ballots held in November 1860 were as follows:

	Yes	No
The Marches	133,765	1212
Umbria	97,040	360

The speed with which Cavour had plebiscites organised and the extent to which they were, again, fixed is evidence of his political effectiveness. In reality, Garibaldi was outmanoeuvred.

From 3 October 1860, the Piedmontese army was led in person by Victor Emmanuel. On 26 October, **Garibaldi and Victor Emmanuel** met at the head of the two armies at Teano. A triumphal entry of Naples was stage-managed on 7 November, and Garibaldi formally handed his conquests over to the King. Thereafter, Garibaldi was politically isolated despite the fact he had just completed

Garibaldi and the King
Despite entering Naples together in triumph in November 1860, the two parted on bad terms. The King refused to inspect Garibaldi's army of Red Shirts, despite their loyalty. In return, Garibaldi refused titles and pensions. He opted instead for a year's supply of macaroni as a reward.

the conquest of nearly half of the Italian peninsula in the name of the Piedmontese king! In Piedmont, Garibaldi was not portrayed as a hero but as an illiberal, authoritarian figure. Indeed, he helped to encourage this image by asking for special powers to rule the south for another year. These were refused. So he left for his island home of Caprera promising, rather ominously for Victor Emmanuel, to return to free Rome and Venice, which were still in foreign hands.

WHAT WAS THE FOREIGN REACTION TO ITALIAN UNITY?

There was a mixed reaction amongst the foreign powers to events in Italy. A meeting of the rulers of Austria, Prussia and Russia in Warsaw received the news of Piedmontese expansion coolly. It was even suggested at the meeting that Austrian forces might invade Lombardy whilst Piedmontese forces were engaged in the south. This plan came to nothing and no foreign power went so far as to order military intervention in what most considered an Italian 'revolution'. However, the events of the summer of 1860 had raised diplomatic tension and most powers reacted in one way or another.

Austria Fearful that the tide of Italian patriotism might spread to Venice, Austria reinforced its armed forces in the region.

Russia In protest at the unseating of the ruling House of Bourbon in Naples, the Russians broke off diplomatic relations with Piedmont.

France Conscious as ever of Catholic opinion in France, Louis Napoleon expressed concern that the Papacy was under threat.

Britain The British Prime Minister, Lord Palmerston, and the Foreign Secretary, Lord John Russell, were keen to deter the intervention of any of the major European powers in the unification process. British suspicion of Louis Napoleon's intentions were increased by the annexation of Nice and Savoy in March 1860. The prospect of Austria, Russia and Prussia combining to act, provoked the issuing of a public note from the British government on 27 October 1860. The note was to have an important impact on the situation. In the note the British government gave their support to the newly unified state which had, according to Russell who was the author of the note, come about by '*a people building up the edifice of their liberties*'.

In a second note Russell attacked the despotic rule of the Papal States and the Kingdom of Naples and warned that if any foreign power intervened in the new state then Britain would intervene militarily. This note, however, was not issued because of the misgivings of Queen Victoria who had sympathy with Austria. In the end this proved not to be of any great significance, the support expressed in the first note was a sufficient guarantee for the new state.

CONCLUSION

Italy had been unified through a number of factors.

- The impact of foreign powers should not be underestimated nor should the diplomacy of Cavour and his use of the National Society be overlooked.
- Cavour was one of the central characters of the unification process. His contribution to the economic modernisation of Piedmont was especially significant.
- As a diplomat, Cavour was often forced to respond to events as much as provoke change. However, his consummate skill, especially in the critical years 1859 and 1860, were of fundamental importance in shaping the Italian nation.
- However, Cavour should not be considered an Italian nationalist. He was primarily a political pragmatist.
- Garibaldi's significance was to turn the unification of the northern regions of Italy into unification of the whole peninsula. It was also to act as a thorn in the side of the more cautious conservatives.

Reflections on Cavour In the biography *Cavour* (1985), Denis Mack Smith paints a portrait of Cavour as an architect of the unification of Italy. According to Mack Smith, Cavour was the arch diplomat and a brilliant political operator. He also identified Cavour's great strength as the ability to manage Parliament. Indeed, the forging of the *connubio* was Cavour's master trick. It gave him the legitimacy of Parliamentary support for his actions and from that support he derived his considerable authority.

In one of the most enlightening sections of his book, Mack Smith identified that Cavour was a bundle of contradictions. On the one hand he was a conservative, but on the other he occasionally resorted to revolutionary action. He could also be idealistic and cynical, kind but ruthless, cautious and occasionally audacious. Mack Smith also stresses Cavour's '*ability to manage parliament... [skill] in foreign policy and... sheer virtuosity in every branch of the political arts*'. This list is undoubtedly accurate.

ACTIVITY

Below are two sources, both written by Cavour in 1860. Read through the sources and answer the following questions:

- What do these sources tell us about Cavour's concerns and intentions?
- How reliable are these extracts for an historian?

Enquiries

Study Sources A and B

Compare these Sources as evidence for Cavour's reaction to Garibaldi's actions in 1860.

Source A: Cavour clearly expresses the difficulty of his situation.

[Garibaldi] *cannot be stopped from making war on the Kingdom of Naples. It may be good, it may be bad, but it was inevitable. If we had tried to restrain Garibaldi by force he would have become a real domestic problem. Now what will happen? It is impossible to predict. Will England help him? It is possible. Will France oppose him? I don't think so. And what about us? We cannot support him openly, nor can we encourage private efforts on his behalf. We have therefore decided not to allow any more sailings from Genoa or Livorno, but also not to prevent the dispatch of arms and ammunition, provided they are sent off with a certain prudence. I fully recognise all of the disadvantages of the ambiguous line that we are adopting, but I cannot work out any other policy that doesn't have even greater dangers.*

> From a letter from Cavour to fellow
> politician Ricasoli dated 16 May 1860

Source B: Cavour considers his options as Garibaldi threatens to invade the mainland.

If Garibaldi crosses to the mainland and takes over the Kingdom of Naples and its capital, as he has done in Sicily and Palermo, he becomes absolute master of the situation. King Victor Emmanuel loses almost all his prestige; in the eyes of nearly all Italians, he becomes the friend of Garibaldi. He will probably keep his Crown but the Crown will shine only with the reflected light emitted by a heroic adventurer. Garibaldi will not proclaim the republic at Naples, but he will not annex it to Piedmont either, and he will hold it as dictator. Once he has the resources of a kingdom of nine million inhabitants, as well as irresistible popular prestige, we cannot fight against him. He will be stronger than us.

Although we have decided what to do if Garibaldi is completely successful in the Kingdom of Naples, I believe it is our duty to the King and to Italy to do everything in our power to prevent his success.

From a letter from Cavour to fellow
politician Niagra dated 1 August 1860

CHAPTER 9

How far was Italy united in the years 1861–70?

INTRODUCTION

Italy was unified as a nation state in 1860. However, that did not mean that Italy was now united in reality. There were a number of divisions that remained and issues to address. The following ten years saw attempts to address these divisions with varying degrees of success. The most serious issues were the following:

- The considerable divisions between the North and the South.
- The question of whether Italy should be a unitary or a federal state.
- A weak government.
- Economic integration of all regions.
- Divisions between the Church and the new state.
- The unresolved questions surrounding the status of Rome and Venice.

WHAT WERE THE ISSUES?

Legal and Real Italy

From the start, the problem for the new Italian state was how to reconcile the new state, its institutions, laws and customs to large areas of Italy which found those new institutions, laws and customs to be alien. In his book *Modern Italy 1871–1995* (1996), historian Martin Clark explains the chasm between what he terms 'legal Italy' (that is, the state) and 'real Italy' (those who were not part of the new 'legal Italy'). Many Italians felt isolated and betrayed by the imposition of a centralised state that was essentially Piedmont writ large. Therefore, the new pattern of government of Italy that was to dominate for many decades to come was set. The unification of Italy had been from above. 'Legal Italy' would attempt to absorb those who wished to be reconciled. Those groups that did not would be repressed.

An engraving entitled 'The Liberators of Italy'. Among others, the illustration includes Admiral Persano (top row, second left), Rattazzi (middle row, second left) and General Orsini (bottom row, third from left).

Issue 1: The South

Many Piedmontese politicians, including Cavour, had very little understanding of **the South**. Its poverty, backwardness and distinct economy meant it was unsuitable for unification with Piedmont based on Piedmontese laws. An illustration of incompatibility can be seen in primary school education. In 1859, the Piedmontese Parliament introduced a law insisting on two years' compulsory education. However, the vast majority of the population of the South were illiterate. In Sicily and Naples, Garibaldi's invasion had caused the peasantry to expect a better standard of living. Both areas had a long tradition of regional autonomy. Indeed, in the early summer of 1860 Cavour let it be known that he was considering some form of 'real self-government' for the southern regions after annexation to Piedmont. But 'real-self government' never materialised. Cavour's immediate aim in October 1860 was to crush any opposition in the South, whether it be from those still loyal to the Bourbons, the remnants of Garibaldi's army, peasants demanding land or those hoping for some freedom. Cavour despatched Farini to the South with orders to crush opposition militarily.

Brigands War, 1861–5

Officers of the Bourbon army were treated rather well. In fact, by the start of 1861, 2,000 or more had been given commissions in the Piedmontese army. However, the foot soldiers fled to the safety of the mountains as the Piedmontese General Enrico Cialdini ordered that all those found carrying weapons be shot. New taxes were

KEY PLACES

The South Cavour was untypical of many Piedmontese politicians in that he had visited Florence. However, he had never been as far south as Rome, let alone Naples. The first Italian prime minister to visit the south was Giuseppe Zanardelli, who toured Calabria in September 1902. He died a year later, which many of his contemporaries thought proof of the dangers of going south.

KEY TERMS

Brigands Bandits who lived in the forests and mountains emerging to cause havoc when they chose. Brigandage had a strong tradition in the south of Italy, most noticeably during the Napoleonic wars. To many in the south, the brigands were their protectors against the excesses of the new state. During Garibaldi's campaign in 1860, around 10,000 convicts escaped from prisons, many of them taking to the hills and becoming brigands.

introduced by the Piedmontese state to reduce the 2.5 billion lire of national debt accumulated during the recent wars. The result was the re-emergence of brigandage and a war, the Brigands War, which was fought with great brutality and claimed more lives than the wars of unification. Civil liberties were suppressed in the South and the Piedmontese deployed an army some 120,000 strong to deal with the threat.

ISSUE 2: A FEDERAL STATE?

Cavour

Cavour did not always dismiss the idea of a **federal** Italian state. However, the ultimate motivating force in his acceptance of such a proposal was political pragmatism. At Plombières, in July 1858, Cavour struck a deal with Louis Napoleon that linked the promise of French support to expel Austria from northern Italy with the handing over to France of Savoy and, as agreed after the meeting, Nice. It was also agreed at Plombières that Italy would become a federation of states: the Kingdom of Upper Italy which was Piedmont writ large; the Kingdom of Central Italy; the Kingdom of Naples; and a reduced Papal States. The leader of this federation would be the Pope, mainly as compensation for the loss of land to the Kingdom of Central Italy.

In 1860 Cavour asked Ministers of the Interior Farini and Minghetti to conduct an investigation into the possibility of some kind of regional autonomy. Their proposals included a plan for some form of devolution with regional governors and assemblies. At a local level mayors would be elected. However, the scheme was half-hearted and eventually dismissed in 1861 by the new Italian Parliament.

Lombardy and Tuscany

While Cavour was out of office in late 1859, Piedmont acquired responsibility for governing Lombardy. The Minister of the Interior, Rattazzi, decided that the best course for the state was to impose a central model of government on both Lombardy and Emilia, despite the fact that Lombardy had been promised a Constituent Assembly to discuss the issue at the time of the plebiscite. The problem was, there was no common language. (Only 2 per cent of Italians spoke the language; all others spoke dialect.) Lombardy had its own education system, legal system and structure of local government. These were swept away by Piedmontisation.

It was not just in the South that Piedmontese rule was imposed. The government of Alfonso La Marmora had to decide quickly how Lombardy would be governed. It decided to impose the Piedmontese administrative model on Lombardy without any debate and by emergency degree. In Modena, in August 1860, a popular assembly controlled by Farini voted for annexation to Piedmont.

In Tuscany, the imposition of Piedmontese laws was delayed for political reasons. The powerful Baron Ricasoli argued successfully for the protection of Tuscan customs and legal systems, at least in the short term. However, Tuscany was the exception rather than the rule. In most regions, the local ruling class were not able to negotiate with Piedmont from a position of strength.

The Constitution

The election of January 1861 resulted in a significant victory for Cavour's centre right group, which was now called La Destra and which dominated government until 1876. In opposition were the following groups.

- The centre left, led by Rattazzi and Depretis.
- The far left, which included Garibaldians, democrats from Tuscany and those who argued for a federal state.
- The far right of around twenty deputies, some of whom hoped for the restoration of the old order, the others simply being reactionaries.

In January 1861, elections were held for the Parliament of the new Italian kingdom and the constitution adopted in March 1861 was based on the Piedmontese *Statuto* of 1848.

- Symbolically, the king, Victor Emmanuel, remained 'the Second' (as he was of Piedmont) rather than 'the First' (as of the new state).
- As a constitutional monarchy, the sovereign body of the state would be the king in Parliament.
- The Chamber of Deputies of the Parliament was elected on a minimal suffrage of approximately 2 per cent of the population.

- The state's administrative structure was centralised. At a local level, prefects (who were often from the north) wielded considerable power and influence in the name of the Crown.
- Piedmontese taxes, weights and measures and, most importantly, the idea of free trade were imposed on the rest of Italy.

In April 1861, Garibaldi appeared in the Chamber of Deputies, furious at the treatment of soldiers from his red-shirted army. His main complaint related to the treatment of his 7,000 officers, who had not been incorporated into the Piedmontese army as Garibaldi had hoped. He attacked Cavour for wanting to start a civil war in 1860. Cavour denied the accusation. Cavour also had to face the opposition to his government from the Church. Because of the loss of two-thirds of its land to the new state, the Catholic Church refused to recognise the state's existence. Cavour hoped to persuade the Church to give up Rome and its temporal power. In return he could offer it freedom of action. In March 1861, he made a speech promising '*a free Church in a free State*'. However, the Church was unresponsive to Cavour's suggestions. In June 1861, Count Camillo Cavour died of malaria.

ACTIVITY

Enquiry
Study Sources A and B.

Compare these Sources as evidence for the criticisms of Piedmont and Italian unification.

Source A: By Giacito De Sivo, a writer from Naples.

Civilized peoples of the world, you who continually listened to hypocritical laments of an enslaved Italy and who, with a spontaneous surge of generous feelings now expected to see her happy and redeemed, be aware of your deception. It is a sad irony that this destruction of our beautiful country should be called Risorgimento; that these tortures, this misery, this knife in the back, this bloody punishment of every patriotic thought should be called liberty; that this servitude to Piedmont, the servant of powers beyond the Alps, should be called independence; that this debasement of all public morality; this attack on religion, this cynical brutality...should be called civilisation and progress. This boasted unity, achieved in such a manner, is a lie. Piedmont cries Italy, and makes war on Italians; because she does not want to make Italy – she wants to eat Italy.

Giacinto De Sivo, *I Napoletani al cospetto delle nazioni civili*, 1862

Source B: By Pasquale Villari a Neoplitan historian.

If we had first transformed our society, and then carried out the political revolution, we should not find ourselves in the conditions in which we now are, precisely because only a political revolution was carried out...Brigandage is the most serious ill that can be seen in our countryside. It is the consequence of an agrarian and social question which afflicts almost all of the southern provinces. The countryside is deserted, there is no industry, no bourgeoisie, no public opinion to check the landowners who are the absolute lords. The peasants find themselves in the same or worse misery the under the new 'liberty' as they did under the Bourbons.

Pasquale Villari, *Le lettere meridionali ed altri scritti sulla questione sociale in Italia*, Turin, 1878, 2nd edition, 1885

ISSUE 3: WEAK GOVERNMENT

Cavour's successor was Baron Ricasoli. However, the baron lacked Parliamentary experience and was succeeded as prime minister by Urbano Rattazzi. Both prime ministers attempted to emulate Cavour by forming governments with the centre-left and centre-right represented. Unlike Cavour, neither objected to Garibaldi's continuing agitation for the seizure of Rome. In early 1862, Garibaldi set up the Society for the Emancipation of Italy. In June 1862, he left his self-imposed exile and sailed for Sicily with the tacit support of Victor Emmanuel and Rattazzi. After rallying the Sicilians with the cry of '*Roma o morte*', he crossed to the mainland. Rattazzi was faced with alienating the French and therefore sent a military force to block Garibaldi's advance. At Aspromonte, Garibaldi's army surrendered to the

Piedmontese. They were pardoned soon after. Rattazzi was sacked, but his successors were to be weakened by the combination of a lack of full support from the king and weak parliamentary discipline.

ISSUE 4: ECONOMIC INTEGRATION

Transport

In 1860 the state of the Italian transport system was still extremely poor. Whereas in Britain, canal and rail construction and improvement had formed the basis of an integrated transport system, this was most definitely not the case in Italy. Despite the attempt of Cavour to encourage the construction of canals in Piedmont, generally there was little interest in promoting this important form of industrial transport because of Italy's topography and the lack of excess water. A few railways were built across the north Italian plains, and in 1857 the Venetian and Lombard railway systems were linked together. It is clear that the poverty of transport in the south acted as a break on agricultural and industrial development. In the southern region of Apulia, for example, the development of an emerging olive oil industry was stunted by the lack of any modern transport system.

However, in 1860 a national transport system became not just an economic priority but a political necessity. In 1865, the railways were transferred into private hands, but the state was still forced to provide a significant amount of capital. A **national rail system** that would allow trade to develop and would unite the disparate provinces of the country was a political priority. The effect of building the railways was considerable on the economy and Italian society. When the Mont Cenis tunnel through the Alps was completed by 1871, the Italian railway network was linked to that in France. This was of utmost importance, given the benefits of increased volume of trade between the two countries. It led to the development of engineering, iron and steel industries. But these industries were based primarily in the north, and in that sense the railways helped to encourage the development of a dual economy rather than a unified one.

Land

The division between landowner and the middle class on the one hand and the peasant and landless on the other did not improve after 1861. The unification of Italy heralded the sale of large tracts of Church land. In 1867, an Act was passed that began the nationalisation of Church land. In the next nine years, around half a million acres were sold. In the north, peasant farmers bought land. However, in central and southern Italy it was a different story. Land was mainly bought by the middle classes and those who had capital. Those peasants who bought land often found they could not afford the interest payments on the money they borrowed. Additionally, they had little or no capital with which to improve the land and were therefore forced to sell what they had recently acquired. The process of political unification was not accompanied by **significant land reform**.

ISSUE 5: ROME AND VENICE (PART 1)

Rome

The issues of the status of Rome and Venice remained unresolved. At a convention in September 1864, Napoleon agreed to evacuate Rome within two years in return for the switch of Italian capital from Turin to Florence. Indeed, when the Italian government (led by Marco Minghetti) agreed, Napoleon believed that the Italians had given up their claim on Rome. This was not the case. There was a storm of protest in Italy and twenty-three people were killed during rioting in Turin. Piedmontese deputies withdrew support from Minghetti's government. In his usual subtle style, Victor Emmanuel sacked Minghetti for not keeping him fully informed. The issue of Rome after was to remain a bone of contention between the new Italian state and the French government.

The role of Prussia

The accession to the Prussian throne in 1861 of Wilhelm I and his appointment of Albert von Roon as Minister of War and Bismarck as Minister-President in 1862 were to have an important effect on Austrian power. In March 1862, Bismarck agreed a free trade treaty between Prussia and France that excluded Austria. While allied militarily in the period 1862–4, Austria and Prussia duelled for the economic leadership of the German world. Whereas the Prussians preferred the idea of a Prussian-dominated free trading zone, the Austrians preferred a German trading

Limited land reform
Those who shaped the political change did so in part to avoid social change. Cavour recognised that:

'In Italy a democratic revolution has little chance of success. The party [those wishing for change] meets with little sympathy among the masses which, except for one or two sections in the towns, are generally attached to the old institutions of the country.'

zone that would include all German states and destroy the power of the Zollverein. The Prussians won and, in 1864, German states such as Bavaria, Nassau and Hesse, normally under the dominance of Austria, joined the Zollverein.

Venice

The issue of Venice was resolved through more direct and traditional means; the use of diplomacy and war. The architects of change were Napoleon and the Prussian Chancellor Otto von Bismarck. In his desire for Prussian domination of Germany, Bismarck embarked on a complex diplomatic campaign to win support for an intended war against Austria. At Biarritz in October 1865, he met Napoleon, who promised neutrality in any forthcoming war. Napoleon also helped to broker an alliance between Bismarck and Italy, then signed a secret treaty with Austria, both of which were potentially beneficial to Italy. The alliance between Prussia and Italy was completed in April 1866.

- By the terms of the alliance, Italy was to receive Venice for supporting Prussia in a war if it broke out in the next three months.
- To the disappointment of some Italian nationalists, Prime Minister Lamarmora failed to secure the region of Trentino as part of the agreement.

A secret treaty between Napoleon and Austria was signed in June 1866. Austria promised to give Venice to Napoleon in return for French neutrality in the coming war.

'Resolution' of the Venice issue

The area of dispute between Austria and Prussia was the duchy of Holstein. In early June 1866 the Austrian governor of Holstein called a meeting of the Holstein Diet to discuss its future. Bismarck attacked this move as a violation of the Gastein Convention of 1865 by which joint sovereignty of Schleswig Holstein was to be exercised by Austria and Prussia. He ordered Prussian troops into the duchy as a result. On 14 June, the Austrians engineered a vote in the Frankfurt Diet of the German Confederation against Prussia. A number of German states including Bavaria and Saxony sided with Austria. This had little impact on the Prussian government which declared that the federal constitution had been violated which was a reason for war.

A lithograph of the Battle of Lissa by Josef Puttner. The illustration shows the defeat of the Italians by the Austrian fleet.

Adhering to the terms of the alliance agreed in April, on 20 June 1866 the Italians declared war on Austria. Confidence was high. The Italians had an army of 40,000, which was far larger than the Austrian army. However, the Italians were ill-prepared and were defeated at the Battle of Custozza. Some days later, on 3 July, the Austrians were crushed by the Prussians at Sadowa. The Austrians were forced to cede Venice to France, who promptly handed it over to the Italians. The manner in which the Italians gained control over Venice was seen as humiliating. The humiliation was made worse by a crushing **defeat at sea** at the hands of the Austrian fleet near Lissa on 20 July 1866. Although Venice was won, the Italian military and state were brought into some disrepute in the process. The plebiscite held in Venice to approve annexation was even more one-sided than usual, with 642,000 voting in favour and only 69 voting against. The collapse of the system of international agreement was clear after Prussia's defeat of Austria in 1866 in that there was no Congress to discuss the peace; it was dictated by Prussia. The military victory of Prussian arms against Austria at Sadowa resulted in the transfer of Venice to Italy via Napoleon. Of course, this was a mere sideshow to the central issue that it confirmed Prussian dominance of Germany and the relative decline of Austria.

ISSUE 6: THE CHURCH

Temporal power

The most significant appointment Pius IX made during his reign as Pope was that of Cardinal Antonelli as his Secretary of State in 1848. Antonelli's conservatism

Defeat at sea The Battle of Lissa was one of the first battles between 'ironclad' ships. Although the Italian navy had a greater number of ships than the Austrians, the Italian commander Admiral Persano was particularly incompetent and the Austrians found little difficulty in outwitting the Italians.

matched that of his master and it is incorrect to assume that one was more conservative than the other. Indeed, the severity of Pius IX's rule has seemingly been overlooked. For example, public execution in the Papal States by beheading was commonplace. The real significance of Antonelli was to persuade Pius to resist attacks on the Church's temporal power. But in *Ad apostolicae* of 1851 Pius argued that had not the 'power of using force' to support its temporal power. Therefore, neither Pius nor Antonelli were rigid in their adherence to the protection of temporal power. In 1861, negotiations between Church and state about the future of Rome took place, but were broken off due to a healthy mistrust between the two.

Fractious cohabitation

Given its lack of military power and deep conservatism in an age of liberalism and nationalism, it is not surprising that the Church failed to hold on to its temporal power. However, the uneasy relationship between Church and state, aptly termed 'fractious cohabitation' by Martin Clark in *Modern Italy 1871–1995* (1996), did less damage to the Church than the state. Indeed, it acted to strengthen the Church's grip over spiritual affairs. The response of the Church authorities to the increasing state anti-clericalism in Piedmont was to suggest that Catholics abstain from participating in politics. In 1858, a Catholic newspaper editor, Don Margotti, argued that Catholics should be 'neither electors nor elected'.

The Church was not just under threat from the increasing power of the state. The loss of temporal power as a result of the political unification of Italy was a bitter blow. Its spiritual supremacy was also under attack from the advance of scientific thought and theory. The belief put forward by Charles Darwin in *The Origin of Species* (1859) that humankind evolved was a direct challenge to the theory of Creation as explained in Genesis in the Bible. Similarly challenging was the view held by those such as French Catholic Ernest Renan in the early 1860s that the Bible should not be treated as a completely accurate history of events.

The Syllabus of Errors

The Syllabus of Errors was the Papacy's response to the creation of the new Italian state and the challenges posed by Darwin.

In the Syllabus, Pius IX rejected most of the philosophies developed in the nineteenth century:

- He claimed for the Church, control over the education system and all culture and science.
- The Catholic Church rejected the idea of tolerance for other religions.
- The Church asserted the idea of the continuing temporal power of the papacy.
- The Syllabus was a direct criticism of the main tenets of liberalism. It attacked religious toleration, freedom of expression and thought, as well as all the 'isms' of the nineteenth century – including socialism, liberalism, nationalism and communism. At the heart of the Syllabus was the assertion that neither the papacy nor Catholics as a whole should accept 'progress, liberalism, and modern civilisation'.

The publication of the **Syllabus of Errors** provoked an outburst of anti-clericalism from enemies of the Church, but also disappointment among the more liberal Catholics who had hoped that Pius IX was still capable of modernising the Church. However, it is clear that Pius IX's interests were always primarily spiritual and that he had a particular preoccupation with Mary, mother of Jesus Christ.

The focus of the Church

The new Italian state suppressed monastic orders and forced the Church to increase taxation payments to the state. In 1866, a law was passed demanding that most religious orders should hand over all property to the state. The tension between Church and state reflected the declining temporal power of the Church and an important shift in its priorities. From now on, the Church was to focus more heavily on its spiritual role. This was shown in the next important move made by Pius IX. In 1869, a **Vatican Council** met. The main business of the Council was to agree with the dogma of papal infallibility, that is that the Pope's pronouncements were indisputable. When the dogma was proclaimed in July 1870, it marked the spiritual supremacy of the Pope.

ISSUE 5: ROME AND VENICE (PART 2)

The increase in spiritual dominance of the papacy by 1870 was in direct contrast to the collapse of its temporal power.

KEY THEMES

Syllabus of Errors In the Syllabus of Errors, the Pope's rejection of liberalism could not have been more clear: 'It is an error to believe that the Roman Pontiff can and ough to reconcile himself to and agree with progress, liberalism and contemporary civilisation.'

KEY EVENTS

The Vatican Council This met from December 1869 to October 1870. It was the firs general council of the Church's bishops since the Council of Trent three centuries before.

War with France War came
as a result of an argument
over who would become King
of Spain. Bismarck engineered
the proposal of a Prussian
candidate, Prince Leopold.
France objected to this
proposal, fearing an ally of
Prussia the other side of the
Pyrenees. Diplomatic activity
ended with a demand by the
French for the withdrawal of
Leopold as a candidate and a
determination on the part of
the French to humiliate
Prussia. Bismarck engineered
an increase in tension, revising
a report of a meeting between
the French and Prussians at
Ems to make it sound as if
war was inevitable. On 19
July 1870, the French declared
war.

KEY THEMES

**The temporal power of
the Church** In *The Italian
Risorgimento* (1998), Martin
Clark argues that the Catholic
Church was '*among the big
losers of the Risorgimento*'.
However, one should be
careful not to argue that the
failure of the Church in Italy
was by any means total. On
the surface, Clark's view is
correct, most obviously in
1871 when the armies of the
Italian state invaded Rome
and the papacy lost its
temporal power. The loss of
temporal power was an
important issue because, to
the Church, the Pope could
not be governed by anyone
else on earth.

For Italian nationalists, Italy was not complete without
Rome as its capital. In December 1866, the last French
troops left Rome as promised in 1864. Garibaldi again
attempted to seize the moment. In October 1867, he
hoped that a spontaneous uprising in Rome would lead to
the collapse of papal power. However, such an uprising was
not forthcoming, with many Roman citizens staying
stubbornly loyal to papal rule. Instead, Garibaldi's invasion
provoked the French into sending troops back to Rome.
This was not to be taken lightly; the French army now had
the new breech-loading chassepot rifle. At the Battle of
Mentana on 3 November 1867, Garibaldi's troops were
mown down. The failure of the Italian government led by
Rattazzi to prevent the humiliation of those attempting to
liberate Rome led to its fall. The failure of the citizens of
Rome to rise in the cause of liberation led many Catholics
to argue with justification that Rome did not wish to be
part of a united Italy.

Rome becomes part of Italy

Rome eventually became part of Italy in a similar way to
Venice. Bismarck's desire to unite German states under the
leadership of Prussia led him to provoke **war with France**
in 1870. Victor Emmanuel's instincts were to support
Napoleon, but his government insisted on neutrality.

As the Prussian army threatened French borders, so French
troops departed from Rome leaving it defenceless again. In
September 1870, the French army suffered a crushing
defeat at Sedan. The government of Giovanni Lanza seized
the opportunity to take Rome. There was little enthusiasm
among the Romans for such an invasion, despite
resounding support in the plebiscite held in the city on 2
October that showed 133,681 of the Eternal City's citizens
approved of annexation to Italy while only 1,507 objected.
Rome was pronounced the capital of the new Italy.

Reaction of the Church

The humiliation of the Church was apparent in 1871 when
Rome was seized. In May 1871, the state issued the Law of
Guarantees, which was an attempt to define the relations
between Church and state. The pope was given some
sovereignty in that he was granted the status of a monarch;

How far was Italy united in the years 1861–70?   117

was allowed his own postal services; had full liberty for his religious functions; his representatives at the Vatican were given full diplomatic status and would be given 3,225,000 lire a year compensation for the loss of temporal lands. However, Pius IX chose to ignore the deal because the proposals were made by a state that had control of Rome and had seized the Papal States. He declared himself to be a 'prisoner in the Vatican'.

CONCLUSION

So, by 1870 some, but by no means all, of the issues facing Italy had been resolved.

- The divisions between north and south remained. Indeed they were made worse by the Brigands War.
- Whilst a new state had been created, it was very much a unitary state based on the legal structures, political institutions, foreign policy and culture of Piedmont.
- Central government remained weak and was to do so for decades.
- Despite improved transport, there was little economic integration.
- The divisions between Church and State were made worse by the capture of Rome in 1870. The relationship between Church and State is best described as 'fractious cohabitation'.
- The issues of Venice and Rome were resolved, by 1870 both had become part of the new Italian state.

ACTIVITY

Advice on how to answer this type of exam question can be found in the Exam Café on page 134.

Enquiry
Study all of the Sources

Use your own knowledge to assess how far the Sources support the interpretation that the unification of Italy created as many problems as it solved in Italy in the years 1861 to 1871.

Source A: From a letter written by a pro-Bourbon, Pietro Calà Ulloa, who was the Prime Minister of the Neapolitan government in exile.

Piedmontese troops are in occupation in southern Italy, but only thanks to a rigorous and pitiless enforcement of martial law... The Piedmontese have kept Naples under martial law for six months; and Neapolitans are treated by them not as people fighting for their independence, but as slaves who have revolted against their masters. Naturally bloodshed breeds more bloodshed. This always happens in civil strife, and Naples is now the scene of civil war as well as a war between sovereign states.

A letter by Pietro Calà Ulloa, July 1863

Source B: Pasquale Villari was a Neapolitan and a well-respected Professor of History.

The war is over and we possess Venice. After six years of preparation, it cost us less effort than we expected. Yet no one is content. Above all the war destroyed many illusions as well as destroying our unlimited self-confidence. Whose fault is it?.. Blame is variously placed on the political system, on the reactionaries, on Piedmontism, or on the bosses. But this is not the end of the story, for you must then explain how Italy let herself be governed for so long by such men.

Adapted from Pasquale Villari, *Whose fault is it?*,
September 1866

Source C: Odo Russell, the official British representative in Rome, reports a conversation with Pope Pius IX in a letter to the Foreign Secretary Lord John Russell.

The Pope explain to me, as he had done before, that the petulance of the Italian people rendered self-government impossible, and the present movement [for unification] could never succeed; we Englishmen would never understand that Italy must be ruled by strong armies and a firm hand. The Pope then said 'Unity is impossible ... Monsieur Napoleon will prevent it, he wants Naples for his family. I have never been consulted by the Italians for whom I then hoped to do so much. See how they have treated and abandoned me'.

Adapted from a letter from Odo Russell, January 1861

How far was Italy united in the years 1861–70?   119

Source D: A leading economist writes about the reality of unification.

The truth remains that our country is getting a bad name; and if we ask why: everyone points out that we are just not paying our way. If we had not already known the fact that twenty-two million people had broken down the barriers that held them apart and had been gathered in common life and government these last few years there would be very little in our economic situation to prove that fact. The nation remains immobile and imprisoned in a world which is quite out of date. No spark of progress has touched it.

Adapted from an article by Francesco Ferrara,
Nuova Antologia, January 1866

Source E: Cavour writes to Victor Emmanuel.

In my opinion the only way to emerge from this business lies in using greater firmness. There must be no compromise with the various parties, whether these be followers of Mazzini or the Bourbons, revolutionaries or autonomists [those who wanted autonomy for different regions]. *We must then act in accordance without views and at once start unifying the various administrative systems. Furthermore we need to publish our Piedmontese penal code at Naples, to reform the system of law courts and do a lot else to show that we mean to impose a unified system.*

Adapted from a letter from Count Cavour,
14 December 1860

SELECTED BIBLIOGRAPHY

The following books are recommended for further reading.

Beales, D. and Biagini, E. *The Risorgimento and the Unification of Italy*, Longman, 2002

Clark, M. *Modern Italy 1871–1995*, Longman, 1996

Clark, M. *The Italian Risorgimento*, Longman, 1998

Cohen, J. and Federico, G. *The Growth of the Italian Economy 1820–1960*, Cambridge UP, 2001

Davis, J. and Ginsborg, P. *Society and Politics in the Age of the Risorgimento*, Cambridge UP, 2002

Duggan, C. *A Concise History of Italy*, Cambridge UP, 1994

Gooch, J. *The Unification of Italy*, Methuen, 1986

Hearder, H. *Italy in the Age of the Risorgimento 1790–1870*, Longman, 1983

Hearder, H. *Cavour*, Longman, 1984

Holt, E. *Risorgimento: the Making of Italy 1815–70*, MacMillan, 1970

Mack Smith, D. *Victor Emmanuel, Cavour and the Risorgimento*, Oxford UP, 1971

Mack Smith, D. *Cavour*, Methuen, 1985

Mack Smith, D. *Italy and its Monarchy*, Yale UP, 1994

Mack Smith, D. *Mazzini*, Yale UP, 1994

Mack Smith, D. *Modern Italy: A Political History*, Yale UP, 1997

Ramm, A. *The Risorgimento*, The Historical Association, 1962

Sked, A. *Decline and Fall of the Habsburg Empire 1815–1918*, Longman, 1989

Stiles, A *.Unification of Italy 1815–70*, Edward Arnold, 1986

Taylor, A.J.P. *The Struggle for Mastery in Europe 1848–1918*, Clarendon Press, 1954

Exam Café
Relax, refresh, result!

Relax and prepare

It is hoped that you have enjoyed the book. There is much to take on board and learn in preparation for your examination. There are a number of issues to address before you start your revision. Luckily, we have some advice from students who have been very successful in preparing themselves for examinations.

Student tips – Stage 1 the right mindset

Sally

I think that the most important aspect of preparing for an exam is to get yourself into the right frame of mind. One of the problems of the AS exams is that you can re-sit the unit if you do not do very well. This may seem great but in reality thinking about the examinations in this way can cause problems. Some of my friends have gone into AS exams with the idea in the back of their mind that it does not really matter what happens in the exam because they can re-sit next year. This is a really bad attitude to take because re-sitting exams means more pressure next year. My advice is: take the AS exams very seriously.

David

This is really good advice from Kishan. I also draw up a revision timetable. I divide my timetable up into two stages:

• Note taking: In this stage I use as many resources as possible to write my revision notes. I find that writing things down makes it easier to learn the information.

• Practice: I think that the best way to learn my revision notes is to write plans in response to past paper questions and questions that have been made up by my teacher. I also practice writing full answers to the questions that my teacher has given me. She then marks my answers and gives me advice on how I might improve.

Kishan

I agree with Sally. It is really important to give yourself enough time to revise. The first thing that I always do is plan my revision by drawing up a revision timetable.

Sally

I try and revise a certain amount every day. I find that I work best in the mornings and early afternoon; I then like to go out and meet my friends. When I am revising I get up every morning at 8.00am and I have started work by 9.00am. I work for 45 minutes in every hour and have 15 minutes off. In that time I might listen to some music, have something to eat or make myself a drink. I work to 1.00pm when I have some lunch. I start again at 2.00pm and work until 4.00. Six hours a day is enough for me.

David

I completely disagree about the music. I think that having music on when you are working is a really bad idea because you are always listening to the music rather than fully concentrating on the work. I think that it is better to work in short bursts without any music or other distractions.

Kishan

I work better in the afternoon and evenings because I find that I can concentrate better then. I always listen to music when I work because it helps me focus.

Student tips – Stage 2 finding somewhere to work

Kishan

I am lucky because I have got my own room at home. In my room I have a desk and shelves for all of my books and notes. I keep my desk and shelves really tidy because then I do not have to waste time looking for things.

David

I think that I have found the best place to work; I go to my Nan's house. It is really quiet there, she makes me some really nice biscuits and she lets me work at the table in the dining room. In fact, I now keep all of books there. Nan does not seem to mind me being there, in fact I think that she really likes it.

Sally

You are very lucky. I have to share a bedroom with my very annoying sister. There is only enough room in the bedroom for beds, chests of drawers and a wardrobe. I used to do my homework at the kitchen table or at the homework club at school. However, I can't concentrate enough at either venue when revising so I go to the local library. It is really quiet there and the librarian is really nice. I sit in the same place every day in the library and there is a machine where I can grab a hot chocolate.

Student tips – Stage 3 which information to use?

Sally

Where do you get your information from for your revision?

Kishan

I use this book as my basic text book because it has the main points and the relevant detail needed to answer any question in the examination. I also like it because it includes sources and advice as to how to deal with evidence.

David

I agree but I think that it is important to use class notes and read the articles that have been handed out by our teacher. We are lucky because our school has subscribed to the *History Today* website which includes *History Review*. This means that we have access to old articles about Italian Unification.

There are other websites which are free and give good information. I have looked up 'Italian Unification' on Wikipedia which has some good information and links to other websites.

David

I have found plenty of good information by typing words such as '*Risorgimento*' or 'Italian Unification' into search engines such as Google. If there is a problem it is that there is too much information to take in. The most important thing to do is to make your revision notes based on the subject headings outlined in the **Refresh your memory** section (see pages 127–128).

Student tips – Stage 4 writing things down

David

The one thing that, in my opinion, does not work is simply reading the text book. I just can't remember enough detail. I have to put things into my own words.

I like to write down my revision notes in an exercise book. I always write on the left hand page and leave the right hand page blank. This gives me space to add to my notes if I need to.

Kishan

think that this is a good way of doing things
Sally, although I think that your approach can
lead to a waste of paper. I write my revision
notes down on A4 paper and keep them in a
file. If I need to add to my notes, I use a fresh
piece of paper.

David

I write my notes on flash cards. I find flash
cards really useful because I can keep them
in my pocket and read them on the bus on
the way to school.

Sally

at sounds like a good idea. I also use
fferent colour pens when writing down
y revision notes. This is because I can
member colours easily.

Kishan

I have a friend who records his revision notes
and then plays them on his ipod. He says that
this is the best way for him to learn because he
does not like reading very much and does not
remember everything he has written down. He
tells me that recording his notes and playing
them back time and time again is the best
way to learn because it is like learning a song.

David

don't think that listening to notes would suit
me. I like to write things down. A couple of days
before the exam I like to write down the main
points and details onto post-it notes which I
then stick all over my bedroom. My parents
don't seem to mind although they think that I
am a little daft.

Creating an interrogation dossier

The historian is like a detective in that it is his or her job to enquire into what ha[s] happened. The only way that this can be done is by using evidence. However, like a detective, the historian has to ask questions of the evidence in order to find out how reliable and useful it is. Remember that a source that is not reliab[le] may still be useful.

Your first task is to build up a bank of questions that you can use when evaluating sources. To set up your interrogation dossier you need to divide a page of A4 into two or use a double page in an exercise book.

The first set of questions that you should draw up should be under the followin[g] headings:

a. **Content/context/situation**: These will be questions that relate to what the source shows or says, the background to the production of the source and the position or situation of the author of the source when the source was produced.

Here are a few questions to get you started:

When was the source produced?
Was there censorship at the time?
Was the author in a position to know?

Now it is your turn to come up with as many questions as you can.

b. **Purpose/nature**: These will be questions that relate to reasons why the sourc[e] was produced and its form; whether it is a painting, cartoon or an extract fr[om] a diary, letter, newspaper and so forth.

Here are a few questions to start you off:

Is the source propaganda?
Does the author attempt to distort the evidence?
Is the extract drawn as a piece of satire?

The more questions that you can come up with, the better will be your evaluation of the sources. You may wish to compare the questions that you have come up with to the person next to you in class.

Once you have drawn up your interrogation dossier, you should keep it in [a] safe place and refer to it whenever you are evaluating evidence.

So what have you got to learn for the examination? You will be set questions that involve sources but you must know the historical context to the sources.

Revision checklist

Key Issue 1 How far did the experiences of 1815 to 1847 create support for Italian unity?

- Italy and the Vienna Settlement 1815.

- Restoration Italy.

- The Secret Societies.

- The Revolutions of 1820–1 and 1831.

- Mazzini, Gioberti, Balbo, d'Azeglio: attitudes to unity and the extent of support for their ideas.

Key issue 2 Why did the revolutions of 1848–9 in Italy fail to unite Italy?

- The main features of the 1848–9 revolutions.

- Outcomes of the revolutions.

- The reasons for their failure.

Key Issue 3 How important to the unification of Italy were the contributions of the Italian states (especially Piedmont and its aims) and of individuals (Cavour, Garibaldi, Mazzini and Victor Emmanuel)?

- The development of Piedmont from 1848.

- The roles of Cavour, Garibaldi, Mazzini, and Victor Emmanuel.

- The causes and outcomes of the 1859 war against Austria.

- The causes and outcomes of Garibaldi's invasion of Sicily 1859–61.

- The Italian Kingdom 1861–70 and the extent of unity.

Key Issue 4 How important in the process of unification were foreign help and foreign circumstances?

- The importance of the Crimean War.

- The significance of Austria.

- The role of France (especially Napoleon III).

- The role of Prussia (especially Bismarck).
- The importance of Britain.
- The Austro-Prussian War and the Franco-Prussian War.

The question that you will probably ask is: how am I going to learn all of this?

The first point to make is that people revise in different ways. You should attempt to adopt a system or systems that suit you best. Here are some suggestions:

Getting started

Student tips

How to deal with the information

Here are some examples of Sally's revision notes from the first bullet point of Key Issue 3.

The Development of Piedmont.

- What was the importance of the Statuto?

- How did the political system develop?

- What were the main economic developments in Piedmont?

- How was Piedmont different to other Italian states?

Sally

I always make revision notes. The most important part of the revision notes is to come up with questions to ask of the information. This means that I am thinking about the information all of the time rather than simply writing points down.

Kishan

Sally, this is a very good idea and I try and do the same thing when I am revising. I ask questions of the information. I then split my answers to the questions set into two sections:

- main points of analysis
- detail

This means that I have got the answers at my fingertips and the detail to back up my answers. I try to keep both to a minimum and I also try to write in shorthand because I do not want my notes to be too long.

Here are Kishan's notes to Sally's point: **What was the importance of the *Statuto*?**

Main points:

- The Statuto meant that Piedmont had a more liberal constitution that any other region of Italy — included certain civil liberties and rights.

- Liberal constitution attracted liberals and nationalists to Piedmont and Piedmont became the centre of nationalist sentiment.

- Statuto also important for economic development.

Detail:

- Laws passed by the king in Parliament.

- Parliament: Chambers of Deputies — elected, Senate — nominated.

- Legislation on taxes would be introduced by the elected chamber of Parliament.

- Free press, some civil liberties.

- 30,000 exiles (liberals and nationalists) move to Piedmont including economist Francesco Ferrara and writer Giuseppe Massari.

Skills focus: Comparing evidence (Part A questions)

Study Sources A and B

Compare these Sources as evidence for the strength of desire to restore the Ancien Regime in the Italian states in 1815.

Source A: An appeal in 1814 by Milanese aristocrat and liberal Count Federico Confalonieri to British Foreign Minister Lord Castlereagh. Confalonieri was a liberal who had opposed Napoleonic rule but was desperate to avoid the return of Austrian domination.

If our country has never enjoyed the advantages of political and national life, in the last twenty years it has learnt to desire them. We have intelligence, energy, passion, a wider experience of political matters and a greater love of our country and we have learnt to fight. On the one hand, we are no longer the same people who, twenty years ago were happy and lethargic under the paternal rule of Austria; on the other, while I should not like to be too bold in my assertion, I fear that perhaps the Austrian government is no longer the same. Moreover, it will not escape you that nature, language and customs limit all countries and impose boundaries and special laws on them. The history of the whole past century has shown how poorly Austria has been able to protect our land.

Source B: A report from Cardinal Ercole Consalvi to Pope Pius VII dated May 1815. The Cardinal is reporting back on a discussion held with Prince Metternich about the restoration of Papal rule in central Italy.

Starting as always from his principle that we are being given the Legations [Ferrara, Bologna, Romagna], not having them restored to us, the Prince [Metternich] told me that Ferrara is being given [to the Papacy] on condition that Austrian garrisons should be stationed both there and at Comacchio. I objected to this on the grounds that the Pope was an independent sovereign but this objection was not considered valid since Austria as donor is clearly allowed to attach rules to her gift. We have decided to call these towns "frontier fortresses".

The Prince also argued that the three provinces [of the Legations]…accustomed for about twenty-five years now to a system of government very different to Papal rule…could not be brought under the old system of government. In my reply I established that whatever the Holy Father was obliged to do in the three Legations he would have to do in the rest of his states. The Prince agreed, and so this was ruled out.

Examiner's tips

How might you answer this question?

The first question on the AS examination paper like the one above is focussed on the comparison of evidence. You need your own knowledge to answer the question because you need to understand the context within which it was produced. However, the main comparative focus in the question is on the evidence provided on an issue and its relative quality rather than knowledge of the period generally.

There are 30 marks for these questions. The breakdown of marks is as follows:

Historical knowledge and communication – 6 marks

To be awarded these marks you need to do the following:
- use appropriate historical terms
- use accurate and relevant knowledge
- clearly and coherently structure your answer.

Analysis and concepts – 8 marks

To be awarded these marks you need to do the following:
- use appropriate historical terms
- be analytical throughout the answer
- make a developed comparison and judgement
- show a clear and accurate understanding of key concepts relevant to analysis and to the topic
- show a clear and accurate understanding of the significance of issues in their historical context.

Enquiry: analysis and evaluation of source material – 16 marks
To be awarded these marks you need to do the following:

- focus your response on a comparison and/or contrast of both content and provenance
- evaluate qualities such as reliability, completeness, consistency, typicality, and especially utility, in relation to the question.
- So in short, you have to do the following:
- write analytically throughout your answer
- structure your answer clearly
- evaluate the evidence throughout.

Examiner's tips

Structuring an answer

This is where your interrogation dossier comes in handy. You need to compare the sources. Here are some handy hints:

Cross-reference the sources throughout. Do not fall into the trap of dealing with one source for the first half of the answer, then dealing with the other source and attempting to cross reference at the end.

Weigh up the sources Although you will not have time in the examination to draw the following chart as part of a plan, it is useful to have it in the back of your mind when you are answering the question.

The chart has been filled in with some points that could be used to provide a full response to the question above. It should be noted that these points are just examples.

What other points would you make?

	Points of comparability	Points of difference
Content/ context/ situation of Sources A and B	**Context** The context of both Sources is similar; both are from the discussions over the future of Italy. Both are representative of opinion; liberal and reaction, and in that sense both are useful. **Situation** Both authors are in a position to know, given their influence and access to the main decision makers. Hence both sources are potentially highly useful.	**Content** Whereas Source A strongly rules out the restoration of Austrian influence, Source B implicitly accepts Metternich's direction with some reservations. There are clear differences in content between the two sources.
Purpose/ nature of Sources A and B	**Nature** Even though there are differences between the sources, the nature of both is similar; both are accounts of discussions held between Italian interests and foreign powers.	**Purpose** The purpose of the sources differs; Source A is a direct appeal attempting to persuade Castlereagh whereas Source B is a report back to the Papacy attempting to justify decisions that have been made. The reliability of Source A is potentially greater than Source B in which Cardinal Consalvi seems to be boosting his own reputation as much as the wider issues.

Timing You will have only half an hour in the examination to answer the question. Therefore you will need to keep the number of points on your plan to a minimum and your paragraphs short.

Structure The structure for your whole response is essentially provided for you by the above chart. Here is a suggested paragraph structure:

Introduction Identify in two sentences the main points of comparison between the sources.

Paragraph 1 Content An analytical evaluation comparing the content of the sources in the light of the question.

Paragraph 2 Context/Situation An analytical evaluation comparing the context/ situation of both authors.

Paragraph 3 Purpose/nature An analytical evaluation comparing the purpose/ nature of the sources.

Conclusion A summary of the relative utility and reliability of the sources in light of the above.

Sally's answer

Here is an extract from a pupil's response to the question which focuses on the relative value of the sources in the light of their respective purposes.

The sources differ greatly in their purpose. As the intention of the author of Source A was to persuade Lord Castlereagh to help prevent the re-establishment of Austrian power in the Italian peninsular it is not surprising that he gives the impression that the reintroduction of the ancient regime would be unsuitable. Equally, it is not surprising that the author of Source B, given the Papacy's desire for restoration of the old order, should be prepared to enter into discussions with the Austrians. However, there is a subtle difference in the purpose of the two sources; whilst Source A is a clear attempt at persuasion, the Cardinal in Source B is not only reporting back on the progress of negotiations. He is also attempting to justify his role in discussions with Prince Metternich and this makes the source less reliable as an account. It is this difference which makes Source A potentially more useful when considering reactions to the possible restoration of the Ancien Regime.

Examiner's comments

The candidate has responded well to this question in this extract. She has argued the relative value of the sources in the light of the purpose of each. The candidate does particularly well to come to a clear judgement. Note how the candidate takes the sources together rather than simply explaining them one by one. The key to the response is in the comparison of the sources throughout.

Examiner's comments

- For AO1a the candidate achieves Level IA because of the accurate use of historical terminology and the answer is clearly structured and coherent.

- For AO1b the answer is also awarded Level IA because it is consistently analytical with a developed comparison and judgement as well as a clear understanding of the key concepts.

- For AO2 the response provides a focussed comparison of purpose and attempts to evaluate relative utility. For that reason it is awarded the top Level IA.

Skills focus: Making a judgement based on the sources and your own knowledge (Part B questions)

Study all the Sources.

Use your own knowledge to assess how far the Sources below support the interpretation that Mazzini's ideas had a minimal impact in the period 1829 to 1849.

Source A: Massimo D'Azeglio recalls Milan in the 1830s. His recollections were published in 1868.

That of Young Italy was a bad example and an evil school for Italy, from the absurdity of its political principles, the stupidity of its intentions, the perversity of its means, and lastly, on account of the mean behaviour of its leaders, who, while themselves in a place of perfect safety, sent to the scaffold the generous fools who did not understand that their heads were offered up not to regenerate Italy, but only to revive a withered sectarian zeal.

Massimo D'Azeglio recalls, 1868

Source B: The programme of Young Italy written by Giuseppe Mazzini.

Young Italy is the brotherhood of Italians who believe in a law of progress and duty – are convinced that Italy is called to be a nation – that the failure of past attempts is due not to weakness, but to the poor leadership of the revolutionary parties – that the secret of strength lies in constancy and united effort. Young Italy stands for republic and [national] unity. Convinced that Italy can free herself by her own strength... Young Italy is resolved to take advantage of foreign events, but not to allow the time and character of insurrection to depend on them.

Giuseppe Mazzini, *The programme of Young Italy*, 1831

Source C: By Carlo Cattaneo who shared Mazzini's belief in democracy and republicanism. He played a leading part in the 1848 revolutions. However he doubted Mazzini's desire for a unitary state, instead arguing for a more federal solution.

The dream of many, but still a dream, is that a single law for all Italy can be improvised by the wave of a magic wand. No! For many generations in Turin, Parma, Rome, Naples, Sicily signed contracts and customary rights based on ancient and modern laws will continue. ...The quality of our cities is the work of centuries and distant events; its causes are more ancient than any memory. Whoever ignores this love of the individual patria in Italy will always build on sand...the general structure must not invade the local structure.

Source D: From a letter from Giuseppe Mazzini to Nicola Fabrizi, 30 November 1843.

When I wrote to you a long time ago saying 'Alone you can do nothing', do you think I meant to accuse you of not knowing what to do? No; I was accusing the Italians between you and me, I do not respect them. I knew that they would promise money both to you and me, but would not give any; that they would promise to act but would do nothing. Can't you see that they are prepared to be defeated one by one? Can't you see that if they were real men they would have acted en masse, at least in the Papal States, when Muratori was at the gates of Bologna with his armed band. I have no respect for my compatriots.

In G. Mazzini, *Epistolario*, xxiv [10, xiv]

Source E: From the satirical journal Il Don Pirlone, issued in Rome during the Roman Republic in 1849. In this cartoon, the Mazzinian inspired Roman Republic, Roman wolf at her side, heralds the dawn of Italian unity by ringing a bell in the shape of a cap of liberty. Pope Pius IX and Charles Albert of Savoy are among those discomfited by the bell's sound.

Examiner's tips

How might you answer this question?

You will have an hour in the examination to answer this question. It is worth 70 marks. This is how the marks are broken down and what you are awarded marks for.

Historical knowledge and communication – 10 marks

To be awarded these marks you need to do the following:

- use appropriate historical terms

- use accurate and relevant knowledge

- clearly and coherently structure your answer.

Examiner's tips – cont.

Analysis and concepts – 12 marks

To be awarded these marks you need to do the following:

- use appropriate historical terms
- be analytical throughout the answer
- make a developed comparison and judgement
- show a clear and accurate understanding of key concepts relevant to analysis and to the topic
- show a clear and accurate understanding of the significance of issues in their historical context.

Enquiry: analysis and evaluation of source material – 28 marks

To be awarded these marks you need to do the following:

- focus your response on a comparison and/or contrast of both content and provenance
- evaluate qualities such as reliability, completeness, consistency, typicality, and especially utility, in relation to the question.

Analyse and evaluate how aspects of the past have been interpreted and represented – 20 marks

To be awarded these marks you need to do the following:

- analyse and evaluate the historical interpretation using all sources and your own knowledge to reach a clear conclusion
- show that the sources may either support or refute the interpretation.

Where do I start?

The key to success in answering such questions is a plan. You have one hour in the examination to write your response to the question so you can afford to spend around 5 minutes reading through the sources and in planning your response.

Examiner's tips – cont.

In your plan you should include the following:

- two or three lines of argument (which will become your introduction)
- a running order of paragraphs (which include the sources that you will use).

Here is an example of a plan for the question on page 134.

Lines of argument

- Mazzini's ideas little more than an ideal and, as a result had little impact.
- His ideas were seen by contemporaries as revolutionary and impractical and their appeal was not wide.
- However, Mazzini's ideas did, from time to time, have an impact; both on other thinkers and on political developments.

Running order

Para. 1 Contemporary rejection of ideas – Sources A, C

Para. 2 Ideas just ideals – Source B

Para. 3 Too revolutionary – Sources A, C, D

Para. 4 Lack of impact – Sources D, C

Para 5 Some impact – Source E

Conclusion

How do I structure my response?

The sources must dominate the response. However, they must be placed in the context of an argument. Below is a suggested paragraph structure that encourages both analysis and source work.

Argue At the start of the paragraph you should present a line of argument. The best way to do this is to use the language of argument:

One should argue that…

It is clear that…

Fundamentally…

Without doubt…

Try and avoid a descriptive start because this will lead to a descriptive paragraph.

Explain. The next sentence or so of each paragraph will explain that line of argument.

Evidence. This is the biggest section in each paragraph. You should look to use two different types of evidence at this point in the paragraph.

- Sources At this point you should use the sources as evidence to back up the point you make. As part of this process you should use the sources for information but also evaluate, cross reference and interpret the sources.

- Own knowledge You should also use your own knowledge (facts, statistics, names, events, references to historians) to back up your arguments. This evidence needs to be accurate, well selected and relevant.

Reiterate. The last half sentence should be a reiteration, going back to the main theme/argument of the paragraph.

An example

Here is an extract from a student's response to the above question.

Kishan's answer

However, it is wrong to dismiss entirely the impact of Mazzini's ideas in the period in question. On occasions, the Mazzinian ideals of unity and a Republic born out of revolution were to stir groups of Italians into action and change the course of Italian history. The clearest example to support this idea was the creation and impact of the Roman Republic in 1849. This is clearly shown in Source E which depicts the dawn of Italian unity to the horror of the established classes. The Source is an excellent example of Mazzinian propaganda from the time of the Republic, indeed Il Don Pirlone was published in Rome in 1849. The fact that it is a satirical magazine does not detract from its validity; indeed that it was published at all shows that censorship rules under the Roman Republic in 1849 were very different to those under papal rule. The message is accurate to the point that the sounding of the radical bell did alarm the establishment, hence the French seizure of Rome in July 1849. The Source is an excellent example of Mazzinian idealism, the events of 1849 may have frightened Charles Albert and others but they did not lead to the dawn of Italian unity as suggested, despite the calling of the Constituent Assembly. Therefore the evidence is most useful in showing that Mazzinian ideals did have some impact although the impact was often short lived and not as great as suggested.

Examiner's comments

This is an extract from a candidate's response. The candidate shows good control in answering the question. The response starts with a strong point of analysis which is clearly explained. The candidate then goes on to look at the content of Source E moving quickly onto an evaluation of the source's attribution. The candidate does use their own knowledge well but there is not quite the range of supporting evidence required.

Examiner's comments

- AO2a and AO2b There are a number of good points of evaluation and the candidate is awarded the top Level IA for AO2a and AO2b.
- AO1a The candidate writes with control and the detail is sound. The candidate is awarded Level II for demonstrating a competent command of the evidence.
- AO1b The candidate is awarded a top Level IA for showing a sound grasp of the key concepts which are relevant to the topic. The candidate also shows a strong understanding of the significance of the issues in their context.

GLOSSARY

Absolutist government This occurs when a ruler rules without constraints such as a Parliament.

Artisans They formed an important section of society. Skilled people and often literate, they were the backbone of any uprising.

Brigands Bandits who lived in the forests and mountains emerging to cause havoc when they chose. Brigandage had a strong tradition in the south of Italy, most noticeably during the Napoleonic wars. To many in the south, the brigands were their protectors against the excesses of the new state. During Garibaldi's campaign in 1860, around 10,000 convicts escaped from prisons, many of them taking to the hills and becoming brigands.

Cacciatori delle Alpi Translated as 'Alpine Hunters', this group could be described as a private army led by Garibaldi. Around 3,000 strong, they were volunteers and highly effective in their work.

The Carbonari The origins of this society are unclear, but translated the name means 'charcoal burners'. Every member of the society was sworn to secrecy in a special initiation ceremony. The Carbonari were committed to the principles of the rights of the people, and were prepared to use violence and revolution as the means by which it could achieve its aims. Although the Carbonari society was an international organisation, it was strongest in Naples where it had perhaps as many as 60,000 members.

Cholera A very infectious disease, often fatal. It is caused by poor sanitation and infected water supplies.

Code Napoleon Under the Code, feudalism was abolished and equality before the law established.

Common land Pasture and woodland that was shared by all.

Connubio A marriage or, in political terms, an alliance. The significance of the *connubio* should not be underestimated. It created a precedent for managing Parliamentary affairs through bribery, corruption and through forming tactical alliances.

Constitutional monarchy The rule of a monarch who is bound in his or her actions to a constitution.

Domestic industries Those industries in which the manufacturing process involved making textiles. Dying the cloth, spinning or weaving took place in the home.

Feudalism A social and political structure based on land holding. At its heart was the idea of service to the lord, usually through military service, in return for land.

Freedom of expression The Austrians did not want Italians to have freedom of expression. Therefore, most organisations seeking change either met in secret or had to go abroad. In Tuscany, Ferdinand allowed the journal *Antologia* to be set up in 1821 and to flourish thereafter. *Antologia* soon became one of the few means by which Italian thinkers could express themselves in public.

Giunta di Stato A group of the state. In this case it was made up of three people. They decided that all adult male Romans could vote in the election and that the ballot would be secret.

Hegemony From the Greek, meaning 'to lead'. It is the acceptance of the values and norms of the ruling classes by a large section of society.

High Politics The establishment: kings, rulers, military leaders, judiciary and Church.

House of Savoy A Franco-Italian noble family, which started in the eleventh century. The family grew in importance through marriage and conquest. Eventually, it ruled Italy from 1861–1945.

Italian confederation This was not to be the unified state hoped for by Italian nationalists, but a loose alliance of the kingdoms agreed at Plombières. The Pope was offered leadership in compensation for losing lands to the Kingdom of Central Italy.

Italian Federation In the 1820s, few (if any) Italians envisaged a centralised Italian state like France. Most saw closer links between the different states being the way forward – that is, a federation.

Jacobins The most ruthless radicals of the French revolution. They demanded universal liberty and, during **The Terror** of 1793–4, executed thousands of opponents.

'King Bomba' Nickname for Ferdinand II of Sicily. Translated from Italian, *bomba* literally means 'bomb'.

Liberals They believed that the best form of government was one that protected the people. Most liberals believed that this was best achieved through the creation of a Parliament that was elected by some of the people. They argued for a constitution that enshrined rights and liberties such as the freedom of speech. Liberals did not go as far as radicals who believed that all people should have the vote, that there should be far-reaching social reform and redistribution of power.

Lower house of Parliament Known also as the Chamber of Deputies.

Low Politics One should define Low Politics as the politics of the masses, of democracy and of Parliament.

Macinato A tax that was placed on the grinding of corn. This was highly unpopular in the towns and countryside, where it was seen as taxing a basic necessity as well as driving up the price of bread.

Maestranze A division of 72 guilds (organisations based on trades), each fiercely protective of its own privileges. The *maestranze* had little sympathy for the middle classes or liberals. One of its first revolutionary actions was to murder members of the 1812 government.

Malaria An often fatal fever that is carried and passed on by mosquitoes.

Nationalists They believed that nation states should be formed by people with a shared culture and identity. In Italy in 1815, there were few nationalists; most people identified with their locality such as Naples or Rome rather than their culture.

The National Society was founded in 1856 by a group of 'democrats' in Turin led by Giorgio Pallaincino. Members of the society were devoted to the cause of Italian independence and came from a range of groups from monarchists to Mazzinians. The society never had a large membership (at any one time the membership was no more than 2,000 strong) but it became highly influential, not least because its membership included Daniel Manin and Giuseppe Garibaldi.

Neo-Guelphs Those who believed in the creation of a federal Italy under the leadership of the Pope. They were so called because in the Middle Ages the Guelphs were a group who supported the Popes in their struggles with the German emperors.

Papal Legations These were made up of the provinces of Ravenna, Ferrara and Bologna.

Peninsula An area of land that is almost (but not entirely) surrounded by water.

Piedmontese isolationists There were some within Piedmontese political circles in the 1850s such as Solaro della Margherita who believed that Piedmont as a nation would suffer through closer unity with other Italian states.

Podestà The appointed leader of a local council.

Regent Someone in temporary control.

Renaissance The term given to a period of European history from the early fourteenth to the late sixteenth centuries. It comes from the French word for 'rebirth'. Originally, it referred to the revival of the values and artistic styles of classical antiquity during that period, especially in Italy.

Risorgimento Translated, the word means 'reawakening'. As a historical term it has been used to describe the development of a national identity, a national sentiment, an awareness among Italians of a common culture. It should not be used to describe any movement for national unification, because there wasn't one.

'Roma o morte' 'Rome, or death!'

Self-determination When a group of people decide their own political destiny and status.

The Spanish Constitution, 1812 This introduced a democratic structure to Spain that was advanced for its time. The main features of the constitution included a one-house Parliament elected by universal suffrage.

Temporal power on earth In the Italian context it is used to describe power exercised by the papacy that was distinct from spiritual power.

The Terror is the name given to the period of French history between mid-1793 and July 1794. It is when the government, which was dominated by Robespierre, ordered the execution of thousands of its political opponents.

The Troppau Doctrine, 1820 Prussia, Austria and Russia agreed that it was the duty of the Great Powers to intervene militarily to support any government overthrown by revolution.

Upper House of Parliament Known also as the Senate.

Young Italy Founded in 1831 by Mazzini, this organisation had an impact on the political development of Italy. The uniform of Young Italy was somewhat theatrical, which was in keeping with much of what Mazzini did. The national colours of Italy were worn in combination with a green blouse being complemented with a red belt and white trousers.

INDEX